Stepping into

the Magic

GILL EDWARDS

Stepping into the Magic

A NEW APPROACH TO EVERYDAY LIFE

piatkus

PIATKUS

First published in Great Britain in 1993 by Piatkus Books Ltd
This paperback edition published in 2010 by Piatkus

A CIP catalogue record for this book
is available from the British Library

ISBN 978-0-7499-4070-6

Typeset by Palimpsest Book Production Limited,
Grangemouth, Stirlingshire
Printed in the UK by
CPI Mackays, Chatham ME5 8TD

Papers used by Piatkus are natural, renewable and recyclable
products sourced from well-managed forests and certified
in accordance with the rules of the Forest Stewardship Council.

Mixed Sources
Product group from well-managed
forests and other controlled sources
www.fsc.org Cert no. SGS-COC-004081
© 1996 Forest Stewardship Council

Piatkus
An imprint of
Little, Brown Book Group
100 Victoria Embankment
London EC4Y 0DY

An Hachette UK Company
www.hachette.co.uk

www.piatkus.co.uk

Contents

Acknowledgements

My thanks to Judy Piatkus, Gill Bailey, Anne Lawrance and everyone at Piatkus Books for their unfailing support, enthusiasm, friendliness and efficieny.

My deepest love and gratitude to Orin and DaBen (and their channels Sanaya Roman and Duane Packer), Lazaris (and channel Jach Pursel), Bartholomew (and Joy Ballas-Beeson), Emmanuel (and Pat Rodegast), Bartholomew (and Mary-Margaret Moore), my own guides (especially Celeste) and other unseen friends: I owe them more than I could ever convey in words. My love and thanks, too, to all of my earthly teachers, too numerous to mention – with special thanks to Leo Rutherford and Serge Kahili King.

Thanks to my wonderful parents for, once again, reading the original manuscript with such love and care; and to all of my family and friends for their continual love and support. Thanks to Gayna for the administrative help which made it possible for me to meet the deadline. And grateful thanks to every one of my clients and 'students' over the years, who have always been – and continue to be – such wonderful teachers.

Foreword

The Awakening

I saw her again this morning –
As shapes emerged from the grey dawn
And her figure, radiant with light,
Stood at the mouth of the cave.
I swear she had not been there
An instant before.

I blinked, disbelieving,
My breath held for fear
That a slight movement of air
Might chase her away into the dreamtime,
As that fragile crack between dimensions
Opened.

I had been there all night
Waiting.
Hoping.
Longing for that brief glimpse of
A world beyond.

'Remember,' says a gentle Voice –
Huge, yet soft, like the ocean.
'Remember who you are.
It is time to wake up, little one!
The cracks are becoming wider.
Now, now, now is the time.'
Hush! Listen!
Her silent words fill the air
In a timeless moment
Whilst my breath is still.

I do not understand,
I wish to tell her.
Please explain, please,
Do not leave me here
Alone, in this God-forsaken place.

Yet I remain motionless
As a rock,
Watching, waiting,
Pondering her words,
Sensing the rhythm of waves on the shore.

The air shades into pink
As the world begins to stir;
And with a tinkling laugh, she softly turns
And vanishes into the crystal cave,
Sparkling with Light.

And only her echo remains.

Some years ago, while working as a community psychologist in south-west England, I reached a turning point in my life. Nothing was 'wrong'. I enjoyed my work, owned a lovely Victorian house, had a lively social life, creative interests and close relationships that I cherished. It all looked good, on the surface. But inside, I felt frustrated and lost. I held a deep sense of purpose, of destiny – an inner 'knowing' that there was more to life than this. I knew that I was here for a reason.

For fifteen years, I had followed personal and spiritual paths – from dreamwork to TM, from Gestalt therapy to yoga, from Buddhism to the Quakers – and I had worked as a clinical psychologist for a decade. But while each had enriched my life, none had led to the transformation that I was seeking. I began, day after day, to call out to Spirit, saying that I was 'ready'. (I didn't know what I was ready *for*. It just seemed the right thing to say.) Within weeks, while sitting in my garden, I experienced a quantum leap in consciousness which changed my life completely – as if life were suddenly transformed from black-and-white into glowing technicolour . . .

In this book, I convey the heart of the Path which I live and teach. Stepping into the magic means walking with our right foot firmly planted in the practical reality of everyday life, while our left foot treads the enchanted world beyond space-time of the shaman, mystic, metaphysician, visionary, mapmaker and co-creator. By blending these two worlds into one, we begin to heal the age-old divisions between matter and spirit, earth and heaven, masculine and feminine, personal and planetary, individuality and oneness. When we walk with Spirit in our everyday lives – when we walk with a foot in both worlds – we

not only have the power to change our lives, but also
to heal our planet.

Stepping Into the Magic is a magical blend of metaphysics, shamanism and psychology – a Rainbow Path
of many different traditions, a path of beauty,
harmony and co-operation. While its roots may be
ancient, many of the ideas and tools are truly of a
New Age. If the concepts are new to you, much of
the book will read like science fiction. It challenges
our 'common sense' assumptions so profoundly that
it might sound quite crazy to you! I can only suggest
that you listen with your heart rather than your head.
Then try out a few of the exercises. See whether your
life becomes more joyful, more loving, more creative,
more interesting, more expansive, when you step into
the magic. Find out whether it works for you.

My assumption is that little of what lies ahead is
new to you. I can only teach people what they already
know, what already 'makes sense' at a deeper level.
I am simply reminding you of what – beneath the
clatter of coffee cups and the busy-ness of everyday
life – your Soul is already whispering.

Stepping Into the Magic is a highly *practical* approach
to everyday life. It offers a whole range of approaches
to any situation, based upon a knowledge of how we
create our reality. It does not guarantee a life free of
problems, but it does offer plenty of solutions!

This is a practitioner's handbook. It is not designed
simply to be read. To change your life, it has to be
applied, to be *experienced*, to be *lived*. *Stepping into the
Magic* is not just an intriguing set of ideas, with
exercises to fill an empty Sunday or two. It is a way
of life – all day, every day. It can transform your

everyday life. It is the choice to grow through love and joy, rather than fear and struggle. It is the choice to create a heaven on earth, personally and globally. It is the choice to fulfil our limitless potential.

May you make all of your Dreams come true – and walk in the remembering of who you are.

With love and blessings,
Gill

1

A Foot in Both Worlds

All the Earth is sacred,
Every step we take;
All the air is sacred,
Every breath we take.
Unite the people, we are One.
Unite the people, we are One.

(Native American chant)

As I strolled along the white sands of a Hawaiian
beach, with the gentle surf lapping around my feet,
I wondered how there could be any problems, any
suffering, any unrest in the world. The air was warm
and sweet, and as the sun began to sink towards the
Pacific Ocean, the sky prepared itself for a typical
Hawaiian sunset of brilliant fuschia, magenta,
tangerine and gold. I decided to take a dip in the
ocean before supper. The beach was deserted, and
I felt a brief twinge of anxiety – but swiftly pushed
the feeling away.

The surf swelled around my waist as I waded into
the ocean. Brightly coloured fish brushed gently
across my legs, and I lay on my back, musing over
the events of the day. I was training in Hawaiian
shamanism with a kahuna, and there was much to

think about. I closed my eyes, and allowed my body to rise and fall with the waves . . .

Suddenly the surf splashed over my head, and I coughed and spluttered as my lungs filled with water. Jerking myself upright, I realised that I had drifted out to sea. Somewhat panicky, I tried to swim back, but my legs were useless against the swirling currents, and I felt myself being dragged down. Another wave splashed over my head, and I gasped for air. I began to tread water in a desperate attempt to keep my head above the surf.

By now, I knew that I was in serious trouble. Surely I wasn't going to die? Not now. Not yet. I had so much work left to do, so many Dreams to fulfil. Yet curiously, I also felt a deep sense of inner peace, of trust, of knowing that whatever happened – whether I lived or died – all would be well, that my adventure would continue. But given the choice, I wanted to live!

Summoning up my energy, I called out to Spirit for help. As my body battled with the waves, my heart cried out, 'Help me! If it's time for me to go, then I am willing – but there is so much that I still long to do in this life. Please guide me safely back to the shore!' Moments later, I felt myself being hurled through the water, as if a giant helping hand had thrown me like a skittle – and as I stretched down with my toes, I could feel sand once again beneath my feet. Miraculously, I was only yards from the shore!

Filled with joy and gratitude, I knew that I was going to live. I emerged from the water with a revitalised sense of purpose, of trust, and of joy in simply being alive. The next day, while sipping mai-tai cocktails at a nearby hotel, a waitress told us that a young woman had drowned that same evening, on the very same beach.

So often, it is at times of crisis, at turning points in our lives, or when we face our own mortality (or that of our loved ones), that we become vibrantly alive, awake, present in the moment – and aware of the Great Mystery that is life. It is at these moments that we glimpse our true potential – as when a woman lifts a car to rescue her trapped child, or when someone who is 'terminally ill' with cancer discovers their power to heal themselves.

At such times, we rise above the 'mundaneness' of everyday life, as if waking from a gentle slumber – and step into the magic, the mystery, the wondrous adventure that was there all along. On the surface, life might seem unchanged, yet there is an intensity and richness of experience which makes us feel sparklingly alive. As Seng ts'an put it, in the oldest of Zen poems:

> '*A split hair's difference,*
> *And heaven and earth are set apart!*'

That 'split hair's difference' is a shift in our consciousness.

Faced with social and ecological crisis – the disappearing rainforests, holes in the ozone layer, AIDS, famine, pollution and waste, nuclear proliferation, climatic changes – humanity has reached a crisis, a turning point. Our choice is clear. We can create a future of doom and gloom, of fear and despair, of lack and scarcity, of violence and destruction. Or we can create, step by step, a future of love and co-operation, of joy and abundance, of peace between nations, of respect for Mother Earth, and creative solutions to our global problems. We can create a heaven or a hell. We can wallow in the darkness, or take a quantum leap into the Light.

Surprisingly, some people are choosing the path of darkness – delighting in grim prophecies about Armageddon, affirming the worst, shrugging their shoulders and insisting that nothing more can be done. 'It's already too late.' 'Let's just vacate the planet when the time comes, and leave it to sort itself out!' (In the meantime, they would just like to tell you how awful it's going to be.) It is perhaps tempting to opt out in this way, to deny our responsibility for change, and indulge a passion for suffering and melodrama.

Most of us, however, are using the global crisis as a stimulus to 'wake up': to move beyond the wearisome notion of a clockwork universe, or the nine-to-five struggle for survival, and to reach for the Light. We are moving rapidly into a New Age – an age of awakening, an age of consciousness.

Right across the world, people are searching for new meaning and purpose in their lives, and waking up to their spirituality. In the past twenty years, there has been a dramatic upsurge in our thirst for personal and spiritual growth. Even those who reject orthodox religion – with its rigid dogma, hierarchy, patriarchy, suffering, guilt and martyrdom – are embracing old and new forms of spirituality, from Buddhism to aikido, from shamanism to psychosynthesis. We are hungry for awareness, hungry for growth, hungry for change.

As this new wave of spirituality began, something remarkable was happening behind the scenes. The wise ones of many cultures – from Native American Indians to Aborigines – were receiving a series of visions. The message to them was clear: it is time to release your ancient wisdom to the outside world. It is time for humanity to 'wake up'.

As a result, countless shamans, yogis and spiritual teachers began to spread their wisdom to the Western world. Ideas and practices which had been closely guarded secrets, passed on only to apprentices and initiates, became available to thousands and thousands of ordinary people. Many Westerners became keepers of the flame, and began to spread the Light to others – and new methods began to emerge from the synergy of the old.

And we began to wake up. As we gently rubbed our eyes, we began to Remember. The teachings of wise ones, of shamans, of channelled sources, of awakened ones, stirred distant memories within us. We began to glimpse our own potential, and know that we had scarcely begun to discover who we are.

Thousands of years ago, humanity used to honour the Goddess, the feminine creative source. At this time, we felt connected to the earth, connected to each other, connected to spirit. Then we began to develop one half of our wholeness – our 'masculine' side, our right side – slowly becoming strange lop-sided beings:

able to think but not to feel, able to be productive but not to be intimate, able to be rational but not intuitive. More and more, we learnt to listen to the bellowing voice of reason, to trust in common-sense and logic, to put 'primitive' notions such as magic, fairies and angels behind us.

As we lost touch with our 'feminine' wisdom, our inner knowing, our true spirituality, we began to trust in external authority – to give away our power to ministers, kings, priests, lords and gurus. As the masculine energy became unbalanced in society, we projected its negative aspects on to God. Long ago, the Goddess was dethroned and forgotten, and God became a father figure in the sky – fearsome, critical, punishing, and above all *separate* from us. Heaven was no longer here, but 'there'. Spirituality was replaced by religious dogma, with separate creeds and faiths vying with each other 'in the name of God'.

As time went by, we felt more and more separate from God – and He was largely displaced by scientists. We turned to science and technology for solutions to our problems, as we had once turned to religion. We came to believe in a world of separateness, of fear, of struggle, in which the physical world was the only reality. Science informed us that life on earth was a random accident, a chemical cauldron which mindlessly hubbled and bubbled, and slowly spat out everything from limestone rock to Beethoven. Humanity was nothing but a biochemical goulash – and there was scientific evidence to 'prove' it!

Obediently, we learnt to separate matter from spirit, or even to abandon Spirit altogether. After all, 'nothing exists unless you can see it, touch it, measure it, repeat it in sterile laboratories' – and Spirit does not follow these rules.

Our inner voice – the gentle, loving voice of Spirit – was dismissed as mere fancy and imagination. The unseen realities began to fade from our awareness, and were slowly relegated to myth and fairytale; and the Goddess within was gently lulled to sleep, biding Her time, waiting for us to remember Her.

It is not only science which has preached a doctrine of separateness. A core message of patriarchal religions is that we are *separate* from God – that there is a huge gulf between matter and spirit – but that through suffering, self-denial, self-sacrifice, martyrdom, countless hours of leg-numbing meditation, crawling on our knees to holy shrines, ritually confessing our 'sins' or taking vows of poverty, chastity and obedience, we just might get a little closer to Him.

This 'masculine' belief in separateness – that we are separate from God, separate from each other, separate from the planet, that the world is made up of separate objects – is at the root of our global crisis. It has led to war, torture, genocide, cruelty, threatening the planet's ecosystem, exploiting the Third World, science without a conscience, homophobia, racism, sexism and more – all because we see 'them' or 'the planet' as Other, as separate from us. Feeling separate led to fear, and fear led to suffering, exploitation and abuse.

The Hopi people use the word 'koyaanisquatsi' to describe how they feel about the modern world – a term which roughly translates as 'a world out of balance', a world which overuses rationality at the expense of our intuition.[1] We have lost sight of the greater picture – the mystical 'feminine' wisdom that we are all interconnected, that *we are individuals but not separate*. And we have created the current global crisis so that we are forced to embrace our lost half – so that we can reconnect with our left side, with the Goddess; because we cannot resolve our problems without Her.

Our 'masculine' side, our right side – controlled by the 'logical' left side of our brain – can handle most aspects of our daily life: getting up, washing, eating, shopping, driving, travelling, paying the bills, organising, thinking, dealing with practical issues. It is essential to functioning effectively in our physical world; we cannot live a normal life without it. It holds our sense of personal identity. The problem is that, on its own, it is rather like a robot with tunnel vision. What it *cannot* give us is any sense of *aliveness*. It cannot infuse life with deep meaning or purpose. Feeling separate from others, it has no sense of belonging. It cannot connect us with the Great Mystery, with All That Is.

Shortly before his death Carl Jung was asked, in a television interview with John Freeman, whether he believed in God. Jung replied that he didn't need to believe – he 'knew'. It is our limited right side which needs to gather information, analyse data and draw conclusions, or to trust in 'expert' opinion. Our right side might choose to *believe* in God (religious faith), but it can never *know* that God exists (spiritual experience). Only our left side, connected to our right brain, has access to that greater reality, to the unseen dimensions.

What is more, our right side knows that it is incomplete. It is a well-practised expert at grabbing our full attention – keeping busy, chattering, thinking, doing, achieving, focusing on what needs to be 'done' – yet there are times when our right side knows it is well out of its depth. When faced with imminent death or disaster, it often calls upon the left side. (In a crisis, even atheists tend to find themselves praying.)

When our 'left side' responds in a crisis, strange things begin to happen. Time seems to stand still as you swerve to avoid the oncoming truck; the tumour 'miraculously' vanishes; a helper appears from nowhere to guide you to safety; or a 'voice' offers clear instructions on what to do. Our right side can think and reason, it has access to information and knowledge – but our left side has access to unlimited resources: beyond space–time, beyond our imagination.

As we open our hearts and minds to our 'left side', an expansive new world becomes part of everyday life. It's as if we were splashing about in a rock pool for years, and suddenly discover there is an ocean right there behind us. The 'left side' is the world of unseen realities – the world that lies beyond the illusion of separateness. It is the world of the Dreamtime, the world of Spirit. Our 'left side' offers us dreams, visions, telepathy, clairvoyance, nature spirits, angels, guides, channelling, magic, healing, time travel, infinite dimensions of reality . . . It reconnects us with our inner wisdom and power. Above all, it offers a sense of meaning and purpose, of connectedness. Its message is that we are not alone, not separate, that we are an integral part of the sacred web of life.

Intriguingly, this holistic model of the universe has been mirrored in the 'new science': in physics, biology, economics, ecology, alternative medicine, psychology.[2] Just as scientists were discovering that the flap of a butterfly's wings might affect the climate thousands of miles away, mystics and shamans were reminding us that everything is One. Our 'left side' understands this. It *knows* that we have never been separate from God/dess. It *knows* that all energy, all consciousness, is interconnected – that there is no division between matter and spirit, between earth and heaven. It knows that we are all capable of 'miracles'.

Of course, in our right-sided society, it isn't always wise to tell someone that you spoke to your azalea bush three days before transplanting it, so that its roots would withdraw from the earth, or that you fixed your car by 'shapeshifting', or that you seal your aura before travelling on the underground – unless you say it with a twinkle in your eye!

At one of my workshops, a psychologist asked me the difference between what I teach and the world of 'chronic psychotics locked up in the back wards of mental hospitals'. When I'd finished giggling, I told her that the main difference is that I have one foot firmly planted in physical reality. I'm well aware of the distinction between the reality of our 'right side' and our 'left side' – and I walk with a foot in both worlds.

In my years in the National Health Service, I worked with a lot of people who were severely psychotic – and they were very unhappy, dis-empowered and frightened people. Many were in touch with their left side, but the problem was that they had a tenuous hold on our shared physical reality, our right side. (Many left-sided people are not psychotic, but they *are* dreamy, floating and impractical – full of vision and inspiration, but unable to put their ideas into action. They haven't 'got their feet on the ground'.) What's the point in being able to talk to fairies if you can't pay the rent, and your relationships are falling apart?

Stepping into the magic means fully *integrating* our right and left sides – which means being practical, loving and joyful in our everyday lives, and translating our visions into effective *action*. It means embodying Spirit.

STAYING GROUNDED

If you ever feel 'floaty' or not fully in your body, or less able to handle the practicalities of life than usual, then you need to ground yourself. It is *at least* as important to have one foot firmly in physical reality as it is to be able to step into other realities.

Here are ten ways of grounding yourself:

1. Breathe out sharply from your diaphragm, four times, exhaling fully with each breath.
2. Walk barefoot on the grass or earth.
3. Stamp your feet on the ground, while holding your hands on top of your head.
4. Lie flat on your back on the floor, with your arms at your side, allowing your body to become limp and heavy.

5. Imagine that you have roots growing from your tailbone deep down into the earth. Sense your close connection to the earth, and feel energy rising up into your body.
6. Hug a tree, speak gently to it – and sense your aura beginning to merge with the aura of the tree.
7. Do something with your hands – such as washing dishes, painting and decorating, clay-modelling or putting up a bookshelf.
8. Do something left-brained – such as sorting out your accounts, planning your routine for the day or reading a newspaper.
9. Do something physical which you enjoy – perhaps yoga, dancing, swimming, tennis or making love.
10. Do something in nature – such as gardening, strolling in the countryside or caring for your pot plants.

In order to stay grounded, our everyday lives should include plenty of 'grounding' activities. (If you don't feel like meditating or doing inner work for a while, don't push yourself. You might need to take time to fully ground yourself.)

GROWTH THROUGH STRUGGLE

The spiritual path has a long tradition of death–rebirth experiences as a means of awakening – particularly within shamanism. Shamanism is probably the oldest form of spiritual practice on our planet, dating back to prehistoric times. Shamans are the mystics, seers, ceremonial leaders, priests, sorcerers, healers and psychologists (all rolled into one) of ancient cultures, and their vision and practice have been astonishingly consistent across all ages and cultures. Traditionally, shamans have undergone symbolic death experiences as part of their initiation: perhaps a horrific 'accident', a life-threatening illness, or a prescribed ritual such as fasting in the wilderness for long periods, being buried alive, piercing their own flesh, or being hung from tent-poles in the snow for several days.

Modern shamans and metaphysical teachers have often followed in these traditional footsteps. Denise Linn was shot by an unknown sniper in her teens, miraculously surviving horrific injuries. Gabrielle Roth, like myself, underwent the nightmare of anorexia as a young adult. Louise Hay suffered from vaginal cancer following childhood abuse; and countless other teachers have (sometimes proudly) recounted similar traumatic tales as turning points in their spiritual journey.

Over the centuries, we have become addicted to growth through struggle. Long ago, we discovered that through facing personal and social traumas, we often discover hidden resources and strengths, or develop soul-qualities such as courage, love, trust, tolerance, integrity and humour. Through 'dark nights of the soul', we have learnt to discover the Light within, and come to believe that the path of suffering is the best way, perhaps the only way, to learn and grow – that we will only find the Light by groping in the darkness. (Just watch the evening news on TV to see how addicted we are to tragedy and melodrama!)

My own training in clinical psychology reinforced

this tradition of growth through struggle. Through anxiety, distress, fear and despair, people are drawn into psychotherapy, and thus hopefully gain self-knowledge and inner strength. Pain is seen as a *necessary* stimulus to growth – rather than as a last-ditch attempt to *force* ourselves to grow, when all else has failed. (Despite its 'scientific' overlay, psychotherapy as a profession emerged from the priesthood and shamanism and – in a sadly de-spiritualised form – shares many of their values.)

Yet there is an alternative to this ancient 'path of the warrior'. The path of fear, struggle and conflict is not our only option. This is the 'masculine' approach to growth, based upon a guilt-ridden belief in our separateness – and it has had its day. Although traumatic experiences can undoubtedly open up our left side, and lead to learning and growth, there is another way. We *can* live with a foot in both worlds without facing death, injury, self-sacrifice, loneliness and despair. It is not necessary to learn everything the hard way!

I'm reminded of a vision I experienced two years ago, while on a transatlantic flight to a workshop. In the old shamanic-style tradition, I found myself being dismembered by a pack of wolves, then lying alone in the depths of a forest for seven agonising days and nights. Finally, my inner guide came to me and, with a gentle but amused smile, reminded me that growth did not have to be so painful!

With all due respect, you created the idea that suffering could bring you Home. God created the idea that beauty, wonder, delight and peace could bring you Home.
(Bartholomew[3])

The trick is to stay open to our left side in our everyday lives – instead of having to wait for disaster to come along! (Some people have a breathtaking ability to attract one crisis after another, since this is their only way of tapping into Spirit.) It's also easy to be spiritual while we're living in a temple or monastery, or while on retreats or workshops – when there is little else to do and we're surrounded by like-minded people. This is spirituality for beginners!

The challenge for us now is to bring our spirituality into our ordinary everyday lives: to integrate our 'left side' into the office, the factory, the kitchen, the bedroom, the schools, hospitals and prisons. The challenge is for us to bring our spirituality – our awareness, our wisdom, our joy, our love, our courage, our truth – into our busy, modern lives.

To walk with a foot in both worlds, we need to discover our own ways of 'staying awake' – supportive friends, inspirational books, tapes, workshops, rituals, prayer, affirmations, notes in our diary, walking in nature, daily practice – until being open to our left side becomes as natural as breathing.

DEDICATING YOUR DAY

Each morning, you might start the day with a short ritual to open yourself to Spirit. You might wish to create a sacred space in your home for meditation – a small room or a quiet corner, perhaps with a low table on which you can keep sacred objects, crystals, candles and incense. You could light a candle, burn incense or hold a favourite crystal.

A suitable 'prayer' might be: 'I wake up this morning in the remembering of who I am, knowing that I am love and light. I dedicate this day to my own learning and growth, and to the service of All Our Relations. Spirit, help me to live this day with love and joy, to be fully present at all times, and to follow my heart.' You might end with 'Ho!' in the native American style, 'Amama' in Hawaiian style, 'Amen' or 'And so it is'.

Or you might like to read a short passage from a favourite inspirational book, or to pick an affirmation card, a rune for the day, or a 'medicine card'. Or wake up to a meditation tape (such as my own *Morning Tape*).

Then spend a few minutes in silence or solitude, thinking about the day ahead, and the challenges and opportunities it might bring.

THE PATH OF LOVE AND HARMONY

Many spiritual paths urge us to ignore, deny, suppress or overcome parts of ourselves in order to 'find God'. For centuries, the religious have denigrated the body through self-starvation, self-denial and even self-mutilation, have suppressed or distorted emotions and sexuality, have striven to ignore the rational mind, or have withdrawn from the 'material world'. All of these practices are based upon our belief in the separateness of matter and spirit – that Spirit is not *here* but *there*, waiting to be found, once we rid ourselves of the minor pests which block our path, such as the body, mind, emotions, sexuality and the material world!

The trouble is, suppressing *any* part of ourselves wastes a great deal of energy, since it creates an inner battle. It's hard to imagine anyone being loving, joyful and full of vitality if they're starving or mutilating themselves, denying their anger or sexuality, struggling with their thoughts and desires, or seeing the world as a 'bad' place to be. That is not spirituality; it is neurosis. How can we spread love and joy while rattling our self-imposed chains or wearing a hairshirt? How can we love others unless we begin by loving and cherishing ourselves? How can we learn to love our planet, and contribute towards global peace and harmony, if we treat our life on earth as a mere stepping stone – 'a cross we have to bear' – to be passed through as rapidly as possible?

An alternative is the path of love, harmony and co-operation – that is, embracing every aspect of ourselves, knowing that we *are* Spirit. This means seeing our lives as a wondrous adventure, a glorious gift from God/dess. It means living in balance between our 'right side' and 'left side' – our feet on the ground, our heart attuned with Spirit. It means holding the knowledge that everything is sacred: every rock, every plant, every creature, every human being; that everything is a divine spark of the Oneness. As we know this, we begin to live in harmony with All Our Relations – and we begin to discover our true potential.

Every religion probably began with this path at its heart, but as we lost touch with our left side, our belief in separateness has hidden and distorted the message. The Hawaiians (among others) walked a path of love and harmony for centuries, until their islands were invaded. In stories passed orally down the generations, Hawaiians describe the puzzling emphasis on suffering and guilt of the Christian missionaries. The old Hawaiians, who lived according to the Huna wisdom, had no word for 'sin', believing that mistakes were simply part of our learning process, lifetime after lifetime:

> *This was a great difference between the Hawaiian beliefs and the beliefs of the foreign people who came to teach the Bible. They believed there was no river, no flow to life. It was a once or never trip. They meant well. They tried hard. They spoke love, they taught love, but they didn't know love. They taught 'thou shalt not' – and they were angry with us all the time for having fun and for the laughter and joy in our lives. They were not allowed joy. Salvation came to them only through misery . . . I am sure their God loved them for all the misery they endured.[4]*

Growth through love and joy was an integral part of the Hawaiian way of life, until the missionaries taught them new ways. (It is staggering to realise that less than twenty years ago, it was still *illegal* to practice shamanism in Hawaii.) In old Hawaii, where people walked with a foot in both worlds, 'paranormal' abilities such as telepathy and clairvoyance were seen as an ordinary part of life, until such practices were declared 'sinful' by the invaders.

As we face this turning point in history, we urgently need to change direction. The time has come for us to abandon the old path of suffering and conflict. The time has come for us to reclaim our inner wisdom and power. The time has come for us to grow through love, joy, courage, trust and vision.

By reclaiming our lost half, our left side, we can learn to live with 'a foot in both worlds'. We can walk in the remembering of our Oneness, knowing that there is nothing to fear. We can embrace our wholeness. We can honour and respect all beings in the sacred web of life. As we do this, we step into the magic, the wonder, of simply being alive.

ATTUNING WITH SPIRIT

Close your eyes gently, and 'go within'. Now find your own way of centring yourself, and feeling connected with Spirit – a simple method which you can use whenever or wherever you like. For example, one method I use is to take three slow breaths, deep down into my abdomen, to centre myself and clear my mind, then imagine I'm in a circle of light about twenty foot across, with my awareness filling the whole circle. I tend to focus at first on my sixth chakra (see p. 112), behind my forehead, but I feel the 'connection' in my heart and solar plexus. It only takes 15–20 seconds.

Try various breathing techniques until you find one that works for you – such as breathing in to a count of four, holding for four, breathing out to four and holding for four; or breathing in and out continuously to a count of eight. Or use a mantra (a phrase or word-sound) which makes you feel calm and centred. Or use a relaxation technique, such as focusing on each part of your body in turn and releasing any muscle tension; or tensing then relaxing each set of muscles; or imagining you are in a peaceful place in nature; or counting yourself down from twenty to one.

Once relaxed, a simple prayer or affirmation can help shift your consciousness further into your 'left side' – such as 'I walk in the remembering of who I am' or 'I call upon Spirit to be with me.' Or imagine that you are expanding beyond the boundaries of your skin. Or literally shift your awareness into the *right* side of your brain. (Remember the *right* brain connects with the *left* side of the body.)

Notice how it feels when you are attuned with Spirit: perhaps a sense of peace, or expansion, or greater body awareness, or lack of body awareness, a sense of timelessness, or a reluctance to come back to your normal waking state. How much can you intensify this experience? How much deeper can you go into your 'left side'? What other activities give you a similar feeling? Could you devote more time to these?

Develop your own way(s) of shifting quickly and easily into this state. Don't make it difficult – it's simple and natural! With practice, you'll be able to reach this state almost instantly, whenever you wish – even with your eyes open at a business meeting.

INNER JOURNEYS

Reclaiming our left side means knowing that our true guidance lies within. A time-honoured way for shamans to access inner wisdom, and/or shift into other realities, is to take 'inner journeys'. In case you're new to this, let me offer a few comments and suggestions.

1. Sit in a comfortable chair, or lie down if you prefer, and make sure you won't be disturbed. Have a notebook and pen at your side, so that you can record the journey as soon as it is over; or narrate your journey into a tape recorder as it happens.

2. Start each journey by breathing deep down into your abdomen and relaxing deeply – perhaps relaxing the muscles in each part of your body in turn, from your toes up to your head; or focusing on your breathing; or imagining that you are in a peaceful place in nature; or emptying your mind, and allowing yourself to 'drift'; or using a mantra. If it helps, have background music playing softly. Relax and attune with Spirit in whatever way works for you – there is no right or wrong way to do it. With practice, you will find that you can enter a deeply relaxed state more and more rapidly.

3. Don't worry if you've never taken an inner journey before. We're all used to daydreaming, or conjuring up memories from the past, or imagining the future. We 'see' what is happening when we read novels, or listen to the radio.

Taking an inner journey is a normal, everyday activity. All you are doing is making it more conscious and goal-directed.

4. You don't have to be good at visualising. Some people sense, hear or feel what's happening on inner journeys, or just get snatches of images – and that's fine. It is very unlikely to seem as real as waking life.

5. Trust your inner knowing. If you find something happening other than what I have suggested, go with your own experience. It is not important for your journey to be exactly as I describe it. Be creative! Allow yourself to be surprised! At a deep level, you know exactly what you need to do. (At least two or three times a week, I take an inner journey with no particular goal in mind – and just see what happens.)

6. Your right side will try to convince you that you're making it up, that it's 'just your imagination'. One way of handling this is to agree with your right side: 'Yes, I know I'm making it up, but isn't it interesting! I wonder why I'm making up this *particular* fantasy?' Another approach is to keep your mind occupied so that it doesn't interfere. I usually give my right side the task of noticing and remembering what is happening – narrating the journey to myself as it happens – so that I can later write down the journey in a linear (right-sided) way. (In fact, the inner world is our doorway to realities beyond space-time. It is much more Real than the 'waking dream' of our everyday lives.)

7. If you tend to fall asleep during inner journeys, avoid journeying while lying down, in bed, in the dark, or when you are very tired, since these are all signals to your right side that it is time to 'switch off'. Falling asleep often means that your right side is refusing to 'come along' when you make a trip into the non-rational world of your left side! Giving it a job as narrator or observer can help to overcome this – and will help to integrate your two worlds. (I've never known anyone to fall asleep while narrating their journey out loud to another person.)

8. I always assume that everyone I meet on an inner journey is a friend. If you do meet a monster or demon – or a grandmother or boss who always terrified you – call its bluff! Smile sweetly, and tell it that you know it is a friend in disguise. It will almost invariably smile back, change its form or even burst into tears. Most 'monsters' are aspects of our inner Child – hurt, sad, lonely and afraid beneath their disguise.

9. Remember to come back slowly when your journey is finished, gently stretching your body, and wriggling your fingers and toes when you feel ready. Make sure your right side is 'switched on' again before driving a car, or using knives or machinery – just as you would after waking from sleep. (You can do this more quickly by doing a linear task such as adding up a column of numbers, planning your routine for the day, or reading the newspaper. Or try stamping your feet on the ground, or exhaling forcibly a few times.)

10. If you find it easier to use guided meditations, try recording your own voice on tape. Or send for details of my *Living Magically* self-help CDs (with music by Michael Hammer) – the address is at the end of the book. (The inner journey that follows is on Side 2 of my *Overcoming Inner Blockages* CD.)

MEETING THE STRUGGLER

Relax deeply, then imagine that you are standing on a beautiful woodland path. Sunshine dapples through the trees, and you notice many different shades of green in the leaves. Look down at the path beneath your feet. Is it a grassy track, or well-trodden earth, or covered in autumn leaves? What are you wearing on your feet? Listen to the sounds around you: birds singing, the rustle of leaves in the breeze, the scurry of little animals, a burbling brook. Breathe in the woodland smells. Use all your senses to make the scene come alive.

Now follow the path, wherever it leads you, until you come to a clearing. It is here that you will meet the part of you which grows through struggle. In the clearing, there might be a tumbledown shed, or a fallen treetrunk, or a large flat boulder. Inside the shed, or sitting upon the treetrunk or boulder, will be a person, creature or object. This is the part of you which grows through struggle. Let it take whatever form it takes, allowing the image to become clearer as you approach it.

Say hello to your Struggler in a friendly way, and tell it that you wish to understand why it attracts problems and stress into your life – and wait patiently for a reply. (The answers will come as thoughts, images, memories, sensations or a sudden flash of intuition. Your mind might whisper that you're just making it up, so be prepared for this!) Recognise that the Struggler has been trying to help you grow, in the only way it knows how. It has been trying to be your friend. So thank it for its help, and explain that you are learning a new way of growing, which you believe will be more enjoyable and effective. Tell it that you wish to grow through joy from now on – by reaching for your Dreams, taking a hundred per cent responsibility, following your heart, releasing your creativity, and discovering more and more of your wholeness. Ask the Struggler whether it will help you to grow through joy, and deal with any reservations it might have.

Once it agrees to help, give it a new job to do. Perhaps it would like to send you a 'wake-up signal' if you are harbouring negative thoughts or beliefs, or blaming, or forgetting to reach for your Dreams, or if you are making a simple task into a struggle? If so, agree upon how it will gently send you the message.

Now feel your love for this part of yourself – and watch as it is transformed by your love. It might become radiant with light, or completely change its form. Finally, absorb it into your body, becoming one with this part of yourself again.

Continue along the path until you come to a waterfall in the heart of the forest. Hear the sounds of the waterfall, and feel the water splish-splashing up against you. Now take off your clothes, and step into the waterfall, feeling the water splashing down on your head and body. Ask the waterfall to wash away any last traces of growing through struggle, to wash away any martyrdom, any self-pity, any belief that God wishes you to suffer – and see the water becoming murky at your feet, as your struggle and martyrdom dissolve into the water, and are washed away forever. Tell the waterfall that you are now willing to grow through joy, courage, trust and vision, that you are willing to love and be loved, that you are willing to create a heaven on Earth – and feel the Spirit of water surrounding you, adding its energy to your affirmations. When you are ready, gently bring yourself back into the room.

While being tossed by the waves on that Hawaiian beach, I knew that I was being offered a choice. Did I want a path of fear and struggle, or a path of love and joy? Would I create a future of pain and suffering, a world in which we are basically alone and separate, with threats lurking around every corner? Or would I choose a future of open hearts and free spirits, a world where unseen forces are our helpers – a world in which our Dreams can come true?

I made my choice – and the ocean became my friend. Minutes later, I was bathing in the warm waters of a lagoon on that beautiful island of Kauai. The sunset was breathtaking.

2

Stepping into the Magic

Row, row, row your boat
Gently down the stream,
Merrily, merrily, merrily, merrily,
Life is but a dream.
　　　　　　(Traditional song)

As I walk out of the West End theatre, I am suddenly jarred back into a more familiar world: shiny wet streets reflecting the neon lights, black taxi-cabs threading busily through the slow-moving traffic, people buzzing with enthusiasm as they pour out of theatres and cinemas, pausing to raise their collars against the unexpected rain. For two hours, I have been 'inhabiting' rural Ireland – enraptured by the passions, foibles, hopes and fears of an isolated family. Forgetting that it was 'just a play', I have laughed and cried with the ups and downs of the intimate lives unfolding on the stage. And now, suddenly it is over. I am back on the streets of London, back in my own 'play', back in the theatre that we call 'reality' . . .

For centuries, mystics and shamans have suggested that life is a dream, that the world is not a solid physical reality, but a three-dimensional illusion. Our left side knows this. Our left side knows that the earth is a giant theatre – that our lives are self-contained plays – and that we have chosen to be here.

Our right side, splashing around in its little rock pool, tends to see us as victims – as little ping-pong balls at the mercy of luck, chance, fate, karma or God's will. It might believe that life is a random, meaningless accident, which begins at birth and ends at death – the materialist view. Or it might believe that we are 'sent' here, being allocated a lifetime according to our behaviour in past lives. Or (more bizarrely) that God provides just one physical lifetime – and it's the luck of the draw whether we starve in the Sudan, beg in the streets of Calcutta, compose symphonies in Vienna, or laze on the beaches in Florida.

The 'wisdom of the ancients' – our left side – sees life from a much larger perspective. It has access to the unseen realities. It knows that *life is a chosen adventure in consciousness*. We are conscious beings who have freely chosen to become physical. (Consciousness did not emerge from matter; matter emerged from consciousness!)

We are not victims. We were not 'sent' here – much less banished here. The Earth is not a penal colony for wayward souls who (if we're very, very good and stoically endure a great deal of suffering) might be allowed to come Home eventually. Instead, the Earth is our playground. We have chosen to be here. At a soul level, we decided that it would be fun. What an adventure, we thought, to inhabit a physical universe, to live on a beautiful planet, and to explore consciousness in physical form! What a huge array of possibilities that would offer! What a wonderful Dream that would be!

Let's forget for a while that we are wondrous beings of Light, that we are sparks of God/dess, that we all come from the One. Let's pretend to be separate individuals, within the illusion of time and space. That will give us scope to develop our own uniqueness and creative potential, our own Spark-ness. What is more, our illusion of separateness will create fear and darkness – a planet of polarity, of dark and light. We can play a game in which we slowly learn to let our own Light and love shine through the darkness, and remember who we are.

And so our journey began, sending sparks of our consciousness, sparks of our Light, into the mineral kingdom, the plant kingdom and the animal kingdom . . . and into the human kingdom. At first, our human lifetimes are brief and simple. We are learning how to squash some of our consciousness into a human body, and how to master the art of survival. We might die very young, or fill our days gathering food or growing crops, eating, sleeping, caring for children and other survival-based tasks. At this stage, we are simply learning how to be human.

Eventually, we broaden our scope a little. Once we have decided to be physical, most of us do the job thoroughly. We choose to experience most aspects of human experience – poverty, famine, abuse, criminality, physical disability and serious illness, as well as the more loving, joyful and creative aspects of life. We begin to develop skills, wisdom and abilities which we build upon in other lifetimes. And we begin to choose 'themes' which will run through our lives – such as learning to love, learning to be bold and courageous, learning to be honest, learning to be true

to our hearts, learning to forgive, learning persever-
ance and discipline, learning to be intimate or
learning to be free.

Once we have mapped out a physical lifetime –
choosing our race, sex, background, period of history,
some of our fellow actors, and the life-themes and
qualities we wish to develop – the stage is set for our
drama to unfold. When the time is right, we plunge
down the birth canal, and take on the part of a newly
born baby. Slowly, we adjust to wearing a human body
again, and begin to play the role which we have cast
for ourselves. We learn to improvise our script – and
forget that we are just actors, that it is just a play.
Our costume is so skintight that we forget we are
wearing one. We come to believe that it is all Real.

Why do we cross 'the river of forgetfulness' in this
way? Well, imagine that you are playing a game of
tennis. If you take the game seriously and concentrate on each shot, you will probably enjoy yourself,
feel pleasantly challenged, and learn something new.
If you play half-heartedly, constantly reminding yourself that it's 'only a game', and looking forward to
getting home that evening, you are unlikely either
to improve your game or to enjoy yourself. You might
as well not bother. One reason why we forget that
life is 'just a play' is so that we will take it seriously
– so that we will be fully *present* in the world – which
means that we are more likely to learn, grow and
have fun.

The trouble is, many of us take the game *too* seriously – which leads us to grow through struggle and
hardship! The trick is to be fully present in the
physical world, firmly committed to being here, while

also being aware that life *is* a game – an illusion that we are creating, an illusion that we can change. When we learn to do this consciously – to live with a foot in both worlds – everyday life becomes full of magic and wonder.

So why do we go through fear, pain and suffering? If the Earth is our playground, what went wrong? Why do we create struggle and hardship? One answer is that nothing went wrong; we simply lack a higher perspective on our lives.

Let's suppose that you decide to join an Outward Bound expedition. As you flick through the brochure, and fill in the application form, it sounds adventurous and you feel excited. But once you're there, lying alone in a sodden sleeping bag at dead of night, with torrential rain beating against the canvas, or suspended from a sheer rock face having lost your footholds, or in a kayak which overturns in shooting rapids, you might wonder what on earth possessed you to choose such an experience! At this stage, you are so 'lost' in the experience that you've forgotten why you made your choice; you have lost your higher perspective. If you open up to your left side, seeing the bigger picture, it begins to make sense again. You recognise that the experience is building courage, self-confidence, trust, the ability to co-operate, a sense of commitment, closeness to nature – and perhaps a sense of humour!

Every single event in our lives – personally and globally – is an opportunity to move towards greater love, joy, creativity and wholeness. However, just as an athlete might weight his or her ankles to build up muscle strength and stamina, some of us select difficult experiences in our eagerness to learn and grow. After all, we don't always go to bright, happy musicals and comedies in the theatre; we often choose to see tragedy and melodrama. Why? Because we enjoy the depth and intensity of emotion, and recognise the learning and growth that can come from facing challenges.

One reason why we love the theatre, cinema and novels is that they mirror the greater Reality. In a theatre, we see the central themes of people's lives unfold with simple clarity, unfettered by the clutter and complexity of everyday life. We see their strengths and weaknesses, their hopes and dreams, their challenges and self-imposed limitations. We watch the *dramatis personae* believing in the 'illusion' of their lives – just as our own Higher Self is watching over our physical lifetimes. At a deep level, we are reminded that our *own* lives are a theatrical production, each with its own plot, sub-plots and themes – a play in which we are totally absorbed, forgetting the greater Reality, forgetting that we are willing actors upon a giant stage.

RECOGNISING YOUR THEMES

Think about plays or films you have seen, memorable television programmes, or novels you have read recently. What made you choose these particular experiences? Do you kid yourself that they were random choices, or that someone else dragged you along – or do you take responsibility for these decisions? (Use a notebook or journal to write down your thoughts.)

What were the themes of these plays, films or novels? Can you see the central themes easily, or do you focus upon intricate details of the plot? Do you tend to choose comedies or tragedies? Are your hero(ine)s browbeaten and martyred, or bold and adventurous, or mysterious and aloof, or wise and loving? Do they bravely overcome stress and hardship, or battle against unspeakable foes? Do they have 'a foot in both worlds'? Do you recognise patterns and themes from your own life as you answer these questions? What are your *favourite* plays, films or novels? What do your choices reveal about you?

Now consider the life-themes and patterns of people around you: your family, friends, work-mates and neighbours. (If you are a counsellor or therapist, look at your clients too.) Spend some time writing down any patterns and themes that you see in *their* lives: perhaps fear of losing control, learning to take responsibility, failing to stand up for themselves, avoiding intimacy or commitment, always being critical, focusing on trivia, being arrogant or patronising, playing the victim, choosing abusive partners and/or bosses, being blocked by fear or guilt or resentment, always living in the future or the past, being workaholic or foodaholic or sexaholic, always expecting the worst, or a myriad other possibilities. If you are honest with yourself, are these patterns or themes in your own life? (It is often easiest to see our life-themes by examining the 'mirrors' in the world around us.)

Finally, what do you admire most in other people that you know? Can you recognise the same strengths, talents and personal qualities in yourself?

(Note: It is important to write it all down, or at least say it out loud. Writing and speaking are *actions* – they bring ideas into the physical world, and open us to change. If we simply 'think about things', we can go round in circles – sometimes lifetime after lifetime!)

RE-WRITING YOUR SCRIPT

1. Examine your own life as if it were a play. What are the crucial issues or emotions you have faced in your life, or skills and talents you have developed, or ambitions and Dreams you wish to fulfil? What themes do you see in your family? What do you see as key experiences or turning points in your life?

If someone were writing your life as a play (and someone is – you!), what does the hero/ine need to learn, or do, or change, in order to make the play more inspiring, creative, joyful, adventurous and loving? Would you say that the hero/ine is hooked on despair and melodrama, or mundaneness and mediocrity, or martyrhood and self-pity – or is the play full of love, joy, courage and vision?

Remember that your life script was not thrust upon you. You chose it – and you can change

your mind. You can choose a different script. You
can alter the plot, turn a tragedy into a comedy,
or just tear up your script and start again.
2. Write a synopsis of your script as you want it
to be – perhaps making today a 'turning point',
when your life suddenly takes an exciting new
direction.

WE ARE ALL ONE

For thousands of years, mystics have insisted that we
are all One – that we are all sparks of a creative Source,
and our separateness is an illusion. This is not airy-
fairy mysticism, with no practical relevance to our
everyday lives. In fact, the concept of Oneness is probably the most practical idea we will ever come across!
What's more, it is a key to stepping into the magic.

The fact that we are all One means that everything
is interconnected – all energy, all consciousness. There
are no 'separate' objects or 'separate' beings. Time,
space and separateness are all illusions – which has
some mind-boggling implications . . .

Imagine that you are living in a huge mansion,
and your current life is the living room. Most people
treat this room as a bedsit, rarely venturing into other
rooms (except while asleep). This makes life simpler.
After all, imagine the confusion if you woke up
wondering whether you are a young girl in medieval
Italy, or a burly farmer in the American mid-West!
Our right side – which connects us to physical reality
– can only handle a certain amount of information
at a time. It thinks in a linear way: birth then death,

past then future, cause then effect. It believes that the past is fixed, and the future uncertain.

In the greater Reality, all probable pasts and probable futures co-exist, all causes and effects co-exist – everything that ever was and ever will be simply 'is'. We are multi-dimensional beings. We do not *really* live one lifetime after another, but pursue thousands of lifetimes simultaneously, in this and other dimensions of reality, in what we call past *and* what we call future – including parallel lifetimes in the same time period! But since this is brain-numbing for our right side even to contemplate, we 'seem' to stick to one lifetime at once, neatly following it through from birth to death.

Our mansion is one building, not a set of separate rooms. If we wish to explore our past or future, or another lifetime, we only have to open another door, and walk through. Some doors might be a little stiff to open, some might even be locked, but we can always find the key if we really want to. Since it's our mansion, we can even change the furniture around, redecorate, build an extension or start from scratch. (We *can* change our past, as well as our future – in this and other lifetimes.)

> *Like a tapestry*
> *in three dimensions,*
> *the patterns of our lives*
> *weave in and out,*
> *among and between*
> *the threads of our awareness,*
> *softly hinting*
> *that within each thread*
> *lies a galaxy of others.*

Another practical application of Oneness is that we can communicate with anything and anyone at will – from a tree to a typewriter, from a great grandmother in Spirit to a far-flung friend. Since all consciousness is interconnected, we can send or receive messages, give or receive healing, or ask for information – all at a distance. It just requires a little practice, and trust.

For example, a few evenings ago my cat Gemma failed to come home for supper. By midnight, I felt a little concerned about her safety, wondering whether she had been locked in a garage or shed by mistake – so I tuned in and 'tracked' her consciousness. I soon sensed that she was not far away, stalking a tiny creature in the moonlight – so I mentally sent her a loving 'come home' message, then happily went to bed. Within ten minutes, Gemma was miaowing outside the bedroom door, to announce her safe return.

The more loving we feel towards the other person, creature or object, the easier it is to communicate. Shouting at your computer is unlikely to resolve a fault, but there are engineers who secretly fix computers by 'hands-on healing'. Crazy though it sounds, try sending your faulty computer (or TV, or washing machine) loving thoughts, or *asking* it what will help and waiting for an inner reply. Shamans have always known that everything is conscious – every rock, every tree, every cloud – and that all consciousness is One. We *can* 'talk' to everything else in the universe, if we reach out with love, and trust what we 'hear'.

CREATING OUR OWN REALITY

Another immensely practical consequence of our Oneness is that, since everything is interconnected, nothing happens by chance. *Our thoughts and beliefs create our reality.* Our thoughts are energy, and that energy attracts people, events and opportunities which 'match' that energy, which resonate with it. Every thought is a prayer. Whatever we believe or desire or fear or expect, we magnetise towards us. There is no such thing as luck, chance, coincidence or fate. There are no accidents. Nothing is predestined, other than our *chosen* destiny (and *that* we can change).

Some people believe that, having chosen our life-script, we simply live it out exactly as planned. This would be dreadfully dull – and would make us victims of our 'past' choices. In fact, neither the past nor the future is fixed. The present moment is our point of power.

Day by day, moment by moment, we create our own reality: our present, our past and our future. Everyone is the script-writer, producer, director and star of their own play. Whether you are promoted, made redundant, go bankrupt, win a lottery, discover dry rot or get burgled, you have created that event. Everyone is a hundred per cent responsible for their lives.

Let's suppose that Jean has a core belief that 'Life is a struggle.' She believes that she lives in a bad neighbourhood, keeps her doors locked at all times, and sees herself as hard-done-by. Melanie, who lives next door, has a very different set of beliefs. She is convinced that people are good and loving at heart, enjoys the graffiti on the bus shelters, and expects life to go smoothly. One night, a burglar is looking for a house to break into. He walks straight past Melanie's house – somehow it doesn't 'feel right' there – and stealthily enters Jean's back yard. Without realising it, he has been magnetised towards Jean's house. Getting burgled would be consistent with Jean's beliefs – so the thief unknowingly plays his role in her script, and obliges her with a burglary.

Reality is frozen thought. The outside world is simply a feedback system. It reflects back our own beliefs and attitudes, our desires and fears, our thoughts and feelings, our choices, our expectations, our family scripts and hidden agendas. The outer world mirrors our inner world. Each of us attracts towards us people whose scripts neatly match our own. Everything is interconnected – and whatever happens is an opportunity to learn and grow.

When we live with a foot in both worlds, then our response to a burglary (or any other event) might seem rather odd to other people. While dealing with the practical issues, and honouring our natural human feelings of rage, grief and so on, we will also ask ourselves: 'How did I attract this burglary into my life? What is the message I was trying to give myself? Which beliefs, fears or hidden agendas created this? What are the payoffs I was secretly hoping for? What was I hoping to learn from this?' In other words, we take responsibility for the event, recognising that we are the scriptwriter of our own play. We devote time to learning from it, and then forgive ourselves. Instead of weeping and wailing and gnashing our teeth, we know that we wouldn't have created such a traumatic event unless there was an important lesson to learn.

This doesn't mean *blaming* yourself for (say) a burglary, but taking responsibility for it – and being intrigued by it. Perhaps you are still hooked on growing through struggle? Perhaps your inner Child still sees itself as a victim, and needs healing? Perhaps your personal space feels invaded, or you are afraid, or you have unresolved resentment or grief, and this event was intended to bring those feelings to the surface? Perhaps you need love and support, and have learnt to ask for it through being a victim? Perhaps you need to acknowledge your own darkness, your shadow side, as mirrored by the burglar? Or perhaps you needed to remind yourself that material possessions are not really important? Whatever the message, you will be determined to listen to it, and to take whatever inner or outer action is needed.

Stepping into the magic does not offer a guarantee that we will *always* grow through joy! However, it does mean that we are much less likely to attract traumatic events, and need never suffer in vain – that we will never use a trauma to reinforce the beliefs which attracted it in the first place. ('Look, I've been burgled! I *told* you the world is a dangerous place!') Instead, knowing that *our beliefs create our experiences*, not vice versa, we will accept that *we* created the event, and *we* can prevent something similar happening again. To change our experiences, we need to change our beliefs – since that is the magical way in which our reality works.

Of course, this sounds quite outlandish to our

'commonsense' view of reality – but we should remember that our common-sense is just the current orthodoxy, which often hides or distorts the truth. Common-sense used to tell people that the Earth was flat, or that women were less intelligent than men. Our views of reality are forever changing, as we learn and grow – and thousands of people, including many well-known scientists and philosophers, are now challenging 'commonsense', and coming to similar conclusions about the Oneness of reality.

Unlike the flat Earth, 'creating our own reality' is a concept which can neither be proved nor disproved – and this is part of its purpose. It lies beyond the reach of logic and rationality, beyond the limitations of empirical evidence. It can only be grasped intuitively, so it challenges us to expand in a new direction. It challenges us to reclaim our left side.

Many people reject the idea that we create every aspect of our lives. (I resisted it for many years, especially when life did not go according to plan!) After all, it can be comforting to believe that we are passive victims of life, that we are acting out a script which someone else has written, or that something was 'not meant to be'. It justifies self-pity, and allows us to sit back and wait for help. It means that any misfortune or suffering is 'God's will' or fate, and none of our doing. It allows us to blame and to punish others. Taking full responsibility for our lives is not an easy option – but it is an essential step in our spiritual growth. It is essential if we are to grow through joy rather than struggle.

Every time we blame someone or something 'out there' for how we feel, or for what happens, we are giving away our power. (After all, if 'they' did it to you, only 'they' can change your life.) If we can find the strength and courage to say, 'OK, I was abused as a child, but I'm not going to abuse myself as an adult; my life is my own now, and from now on I'm going to heal my inner Child, and take care of myself; or 'I've chosen to be black in a white society, and that gives me a lot of challenges – but I'm going to see everyone as equal, and help to heal the racism in the world'; or 'I've always blamed my poor relationships on being so tall/short/fat/thin/spotty/disabled, but I'm going to take responsibility for my relationships from now on; I chose my body, my body is part of me – and I'll learn to really love myself, then we are reclaiming our power.

TAKING RESPONSIBILITY

How much responsibility do you take for your life? Do you ever blame others for treating you badly, or for 'preventing' you from doing what you want? Or blame your childhood for emotional problems or relationship difficulties? Have you ever blamed 'the recession' or 'the state of the housing market' for business falling off, or being unable to sell your house? Have you ever blamed your body for feeling bad about yourself? Do you ever feel sorry for yourself? Do you see yourself as a 'victim' because you are a woman, or because you are black, or poor, or Catholic, or Jewish, or tall, or short – or for any other reason? Do you feel you're 'unlucky' if you have a flat tyre, or get a parking ticket? Do you see yourself as 'catching' colds or 'flu, or being a 'victim' of any other illness? Or perhaps you fail to take responsibility for your successes? ('Oh, I was just lucky.' 'The other candidates weren't up to much.' 'Anyone could have done it.')

Look at where you tend to give away your power, and write a statement taking a hundred per cent responsibility for your life.

CHOOSING OUR PARENTS

Another aspect of taking a hundred per cent responsibility for our lives is acknowledging – however crazy it sounds – that we chose our parents. Before we enter a lifetime, we carefully choose not only our gender, race, culture and background, but also our parents. 'Not me,' you might protest, 'I couldn't possibly have been foolish enough to choose *my* parents!' Yet I believe that we do – and invariably have good reasons for our choice.

As I see it, there are four main reasons why we select particular souls as our parents. First, we choose them on the basis of their positive qualities and strengths. Whatever you most admire or respect in your parents will offer clues as to why you chose them: perhaps their patience, courage, tolerance, artistic or musical ability, intelligence, love of nature, compassion for others, sense of humour, honesty or ability to have fun.

Second, we choose them for their 'negative' qualities – so that we can learn from their mistakes, or so that they challenge us to develop our inner resources. Our conversation between lifetimes, on a metaphorical cloud, might go something like this: 'OK, I need to drop my pattern of martyrhood this time around. It's gone on for too long. I'm tired of dying for good causes, and self-righteous struggling. So will you be my mother, and be a first-class martyr – really lay it on thick – so that I can see my own pattern so clearly that I decide to change?' 'Well, I'm not sure that sounds like much fun for me – but since I love you so much, yes, I'll do it! It will also give me a chance to learn more about handling anger.' And so the discussion goes on.

Whatever you see as your parents' faults, whatever you dislike or resent most about them, gives you clues as to the 'script' that you planned together. If you've never thought about their shortcomings, it's worth doing so – simply because you're less likely to repeat their mistakes if you're aware of them. Perhaps you see their faults as living in fear, or being pessimistic, or unable to express anger or sadness, or not taking responsibility for their lives, or abusing their power, or always conforming to what was expected, or bearing grudges, or not having principles, or lacking vision, or being critical and judgmental. Whatever their faults, it's worth remembering that this might have been their 'gift' to you – a characteristic which they agreed to express, so that you could learn from it.

Once we have learnt the lesson, our parents are free to change. It is amazing how often this happens! Just as we 'come to terms' with our parents, they miraculously begin to change – because they have fulfilled their contract, and so are liberated.

Third, we choose our parents for the childhood experiences which they offer us. Perhaps living in several different countries so that we learn to be adaptable, to respect other cultures, and to make friends easily. Perhaps being abandoned at an early age, so that we learn about self-reliance, coping with grief, forgiveness and letting go of the past. Perhaps being exposed to people, issues or ideas which will form the basis of our life's work, by lighting a flame of anger, compassion, enthusiasm or curiosity within us. Or perhaps living in peaceful isolation, so that we learn to be our own best friend, and to listen to the gentle voices of Spirit and nature. Again, look at your childhood objectively, and see what learning experiences you gained from it.

Fourth, many people nowadays are what I call 'Light-keepers in dark families'. That is, they have agreed to enter a family in which there was a pattern of physical, emotional or sexual abuse, knowing that they had sufficient strength and maturity as souls to 'break the chain'. One reason why child abuse is now so widely reported in the media is that a pattern which has been passed down countless generations is being broken. It is coming to the surface to be healed. After all, if everyone who was abused in childhood refuses to abuse their own children, and instead seeks healing for their inner Child, then child abuse will come to an end. This is the task of the Light-keepers. In the process, they will learn about self-love, forgiveness, honouring their emotions, and releasing the past. (Many children agree to be teachers to their parents – perhaps to offer them an example of love, courage, wisdom or joy through the way they live their own lives.)

A crucial point to remember about Light-keepers in dark families is that although, *at a soul level*, they chose their parents, this does *not* mean that the child 'chose' to be abused. The child was a victim of that abuse. There are no exceptions to this rule. An abused child is always a victim. It is only as adults that we can begin to take responsibility for choosing our parents. The danger, at this point, is that we might use our spirituality to 'understand and forgive' while our inner Child is still hurt, angry and confused. This is misusing spirituality to avoid feeling our pain. Our responsibility as spiritual adults is to love and honour our inner Child, and to do whatever healing work might be necessary.

SOUL-LINKING WITH YOUR PARENTS

Relax deeply, then imagine that you are rising upwards – going up, up, up into what looks like a starry sky – up into the mental plane of reality. See the 'stars' twinkling all around you. In the distance, two stars seem brighter than the others, and you move towards those bright lights. These are the souls of your two parents. (If you wish to meet your step-parents as well, simply repeat the journey.) Imagine that you are merging with each 'star' in turn, merging with the light.

When you emerge from the second 'star', imagine that you are standing on a riverbank. Feel your feet on the ground, the grass beneath your feet, see and hear the river flowing past, the birds singing and the rustle of leaves in the breeze. Use all of your inner senses to find yourself there on the riverbank.

Now imagine that you are being filled with light. The crown of your head is opening, and a shaft of light comes down from the sky, moving down your spine and filling your body with light. As you are filled with light, you become your Higher Self. You become totally loving, wise, at peace with yourself.

In the distance, you see two people approaching. With each step that they take, they become more and more filled with light. Your parents are walking towards you, and like you, they have become their Higher Selves – all-wise, all-loving. You greet them, and the three of you stand together on the riverbank.

While still being your Higher Self, wise and loving, ask your parents first of all, 'What were the good qualities that I chose you for?' (The reply will probably come as thoughts, or you might 'hear' or see words, or recall childhood memories.)

Second, ask your parents 'What were the lessons I hoped to learn from you? What were the experiences and challenges you agreed to give me?' Again, wait patiently for an answer from both parents.

Third, you might ask what you agreed to teach your parents. What were the lessons they hoped to learn from you? What were the soul qualities that you offer as an example to them?

If you need to forgive your parents for their behaviour towards you, or need to ask forgiveness from them, then – *if you feel ready* – do it now. Then see a golden cord of light joining you to each parent, from their solar plexuses to yours. This cord of light symbolises any emotional patterns, any unfinished business, that you are willing to release. It symbolises the energy that you are still 'leaking' to your parents (whether or not they are still alive). If you feel ready, imagine that you have a knife or sword in your right hand – and cut the cord of light to each parent.

Now imagine that you have a jar of healing ointment in your hand, and rub the ointment into your solar plexus, healing your wound and sealing your aura. Watch your parents doing the same. Finally, say goodbye to each of them – in whatever way feels appropriate – and walk away as a free adult.

(Soul-linking can be used to understand and release any past relationship, or to resolve current relationship difficulties. This journey is available on my self-help CD, *Healing or Releasing a Relationship*.)

I believe that we are shifting into a New Age of growth through love, light and joy – that growth through struggle is fast becoming a dusty old relic, the history of which will make future generations shake their heads in disbelief. We are the mapmakers, the dream-weavers, the co-creators. We are in the forefront of a whole new way of being-in-the-world, shining a light into the future of our Dreams, learning to create a world of peace and harmony.

Our primary responsibility as mapmakers is to live with a foot in both worlds. This means living our lives as role models for a new way of being. It means taking a hundred per cent responsibility for our lives. It means growing through challenges that we *choose* – always following our hearts, and living with courage. It means knowing that life is a glorious adventure in consciousness, a dream that we are creating. It means stepping into the magic.

3

Our Three Inner Selves

Be still and know
Both day and night
Be still and know
That dark and light
Are one holy circle.
(Chant by Jokhim Meikle)

Sally was giving herself a hard time. She frowned at me, and shook her head crossly. 'I get so annoyed with myself. I know what I want – or I think I do. I want a successful career in journalism. I'm bright, creative and hard-working, and I get on well with people – it should be straightforward. But every time I get an exciting commission, I mess it up. Either I become ill, or delete it from my computer as the deadline approaches, or I deliver slipshod work which I know isn't up to my usual standard. The maddening thing is that I *know* I'm sabotaging myself, but I can't figure out what to do about it.'

Since we create our own reality, why don't we create everything we want – instantly? Why don't we create loving relationships, a wonderful home, fulfilling work, radiant health and prosperity – while living in harmony with the planet, and with each other? One reason is that we are here to learn *how* to create our own reality, to learn *how* to create a heaven on Earth.

The spiritual law is that we always get what we want – but not necessarily what we ask for. In Sally's case, her conscious self longed for success in her chosen career; but subconsciously she remembered her fear-ridden mother, who used to tell Sally darkly that 'people pay a high price for success'. Sally was never too sure what the threat was, but she wasn't prepared to take the risk. By avoiding success, Sally was simply protecting herself.

The Conscious Self – what we usually identify as 'I' or 'me' – is just one aspect of our wholeness, one piece of our personal jigsaw puzzle. To step into the magic, we need to understand each of our inner selves, and how they communicate with each other.

A model which I find useful – from Hawaiian shamanism and allied traditions – is that everyone has three inner selves: the Basic Self, the Conscious Self and the Higher Self. These 'selves' roughly correspond to the subconscious, conscious and higher conscious, and also to body, mind and spirit. Each self is crucial in our life's journey.

THE BASIC SELF

The Basic Self governs the physical body, our emotions and the subconscious mind. It isn't capable of rational thought. It simply does what it has been programmed to do: by nature, by childhood messages, and by adult learning.

The Basic Self has three overlapping parts:

1. The physical body

The Basic Self is in charge of the physical body. It sees, hears, touches, tastes and smells – so that we know what is happening around us. It also makes sure that we breathe, our blood circulates, our food is digested, our body temperature is maintained and so on, without any conscious effort. If we do want to control these automatic functions, however, we can do so. Most people can learn quite quickly how to change their heartbeat, raise or lower their body temperature, or control their blood pressure at will – which is how yogis can survive being naked in the snow for long periods, or being 'buried alive'.

Gently close your eyes, and imagine lying on an iceberg in a swimsuit – and see how quickly a shiver runs down your spine, and you begin to feel chilly! Or imagine you are sitting by a roaring bonfire, so hot that sweat is pouring down your neck and back. If you imagine it vividly, you will soon feel warmer. Next, check your pulse over twenty seconds, and multiply it by three. Spend a minute focusing on either increasing or decreasing your heart rate. When you feel ready, check your pulse again. You might be surprised at how easy it is to control these 'involuntary' processes.

2. Memory

The Basic Self also stores our memories, our habits and learned behaviour such as how to drive a car, or eat a plate of spaghetti. It stores every scrap of information that we come across, including totally useless and irrelevant facts, such as the licence plates of every car you saw while shopping last week, or the shoes you wore on your third birthday. Everything goes into the computer. We might not know how to get it *out* again – but it's *in* there somewhere! The Basic Self also holds our memories from other lifetimes. (See Chapter 10.)

3. The inner Child

The Basic Self also includes our inner Child – that living self within us which 'got stuck' around the age of four or five.[1] The inner Child yearns for love and acceptance. It carries all our fears and inadequacies, our shame and guilt, need for approval, respect for authority, and feelings of powerlessness – as well as our spontaneity, sense of wonder and *joie de vivre*.

The Basic Self holds our childhood beliefs, messages and scripts – good and bad – and clings to them tenaciously, unless we firmly give it new instructions. If your inner Child was told 'You're no good at spelling', 'Never trust strangers', 'You'll never make friends', 'You can't have it all' or 'Life is a struggle', it probably still holds those beliefs. More than that, it will strive to *confirm* those outdated messages.

The Basic Self makes no judgments about whether a belief or message is positive or negative, helpful or unhelpful. It simply tries to make the world predictable – which means repeating the past. Like a child, the Basic Self likes safety and security, and isn't too fond of change. It needs quite a lot of coaxing before it will abandon an old belief or behaviour pattern, as it prefers whatever is old and familiar – even if it is uncomfortable or downright painful.

If you're used to being rejected, your Basic Self

will be afraid of being loved and valued. After all, it knows about rejection. It can handle it. Rejection gives it a strange sense of security. Being loved and accepted, on the other hand, would be a leap into the unknown – very scary! Who knows what might happen? So it makes sure you are always rejected.

All of our emotions arise in the Basic Self – from sadness to joy, from anger to love, from fear to excitement. If you deny or suppress your Basic Self, you probably won't 'feel' much at all. You will rarely feel sad, rarely feel angry, rarely feel disturbed – at least at a conscious level. Likewise, you will seldom feel joyful, loving, ecstatic or bursting with enthusiasm! Without our Basic Self, we cannot feel fully alive, and will always have a nagging sense that there is 'something missing' in our lives. (One reason why some people repeatedly create melodrama is so that they can experience intense emotions, which make them feel alive.)

Of course, if you do suppress your Basic Self, it will kindly let you know. It will gently tug at your sleeve, then poke you in the ribs – and if you still ignore it, it will start shouting! If you suppress grief, for example, then your Basic Self might create misfortune and loss in your life, in an attempt to bring your grief to the surface. If you suppress anger, your Basic Self might attract infuriating people or having to face injustice, so that you are eventually *forced* to deal with your anger. Or it might grab your attention through addiction – to alcohol, food, drugs, sex, work, relationships – which is a common way for the Basic Self to get its emotional needs met, while also asking for help. (See Chapter 5.)

THE MYTH OF 'WILLPOWER'

Frances had suddenly put on weight since starting a new job. She enjoyed the work, but always found her desk piled high with projects to complete, and felt under a lot of pressure to meet tight deadlines. When she spoke to her Basic Self (which controls body weight), it told her that she had to learn to say No. It was giving her a larger body so that she would feel more powerful! Her Basic Self was doing its best to help her, while also registering its discontent in an unmistakable way. When Frances plucked up the courage to insist on reasonable deadlines, her employers respected her newfound ability to set her own limits – and her weight dropped off again.

Whenever we talk of using 'willpower' – for example, to stop smoking or eat less – we mean declaring war upon the Basic Self. And it doesn't work! Eventually, the Basic Self fights back – and feeling 'out of control', we grope for another cigarette, or stuff down a packet of biscuits. What we resist persists. It just isn't appropriate to fight when the 'enemy' is yourself. It might work in the short-term, but at the high cost of being alienated from your Basic Self. The only long-term solution is to co-operate: to befriend your 'enemy', and realise it was trying to help you all along.

Like a child, the Basic Self's primary need is to be loved. It needs affection and respect, to feel valued and appreciated, and to have its feelings acknowledged. It also needs challenge and stimulation, fun and relaxation – and to have its physical needs met: nourishing food, adequate rest and sleep, regular exercise, warmth and comfort.

MEETING YOUR BASIC SELF

Relax deeply, then imagine that you are in a forest. Feel your feet on the ground, and slowly open your inner senses – see the trees and flowers and sky, hear the birds singing and the wind rustling the leaves, reach out and touch a tree, smell the forest air, nibble on an edible mushroom. Use your imagination. Find yourself there in the forest.

When you are ready, find a path that leads deep into the forest. You are going in search of a sanctuary, a safe place, where your Basic Self will be. It might be a clearing in the forest, or a hideyhole in the long grass, or a dimly-lit cave, or a small wooden hut. Let it be whatever it is. Let yourself be surprised – or simply 'make it up'. Then look for your Basic Self, or mentally ask it to join you.

Your Basic Self might appear as a child, a deer, an historical character, a goblin, a talking teapot . . . Let it take whatever form it takes. (My Basic Self – named Petal – is a silver-winged fairy with hobnail boots.) Say hello and ask for its name, trusting the first name that comes to you.

Then sit down with your Basic Self, saying that you would like to get to know it. You might want to ask about its feelings and beliefs. ('What do you feel angry or sad about? What are you afraid of?' 'How do you feel about life, or work, or relationships?' 'Am I taking care of your needs? What would make you happier? Or healthier?')

Or you might have specific questions about your life, such as how it feels about a proposed change of career, whether it likes your new partner, why it seems to block you at job interviews, or why you cannot stop smoking. Remember that you are speaking to a child-self – so keep it simple.

If your Basic Self won't speak to you, be patient. Perhaps it needs more time before it will trust you? Perhaps it needs an apology from you, for ignoring it in the past? Perhaps it just needs to be hugged or played with for a while? Or perhaps it prefers to 'speak' to you via memories, images, feelings and sensations which you must learn to interpret? (Some people find it easiest to communicate with the Basic Self by using a dowsing pendulum.)

Ask your Basic Self how it might grab your attention when it is unhappy or has a message for you – such as by making your ears itch, or your stomach rumble, or by hearing the sound of a high-pitched bell. Agree upon what you will do when your Basic Self 'calls' you.

Before you leave, give a gift to your Basic Self – whatever it chooses – perhaps a hug or cuddle, some new clothes, a playmate, or going flying above the forest with you. Then gently come back to the room.

THE CONSCIOUS SELF

The Conscious Self, or Ego, is what we normally think of as 'I' or 'me'. Its positive side is that it thinks, plans, evaluates, organises, sets goals and makes decisions. It carries our sense of personal identity, and it *interprets* sensory data from the Basic Self, so that we know what is happening in the world. Without it, we would be totally psychotic, and unable to function. So far, so good.

So why does the Ego get such a bad press in the spiritual traditions? Well, problems arise because (in terms of the Huna wisdom) the Conscious Self gets 'entangled' with the Basic Self. Perhaps the Basic Self feels it is unacceptable to be angry or to cry, so the Ego suppresses and distorts anger and tears. Perhaps the inner Child feels it isn't good enough, so the Conscious Self puts on a front of arrogance or narcissism to protect the vulnerable inner self or – the other side of the same coin – it becomes humble and self-effacing as a defence.

It's worth remembering that the Ego is always *trying* to be helpful. However, its sense of *separateness* creates fear, and that *fear* creates defensiveness, which increases the sense of separateness. It is a vicious circle.

The Conscious Self is rather like a middle manager. On a bad day, the Conscious Self believes it can run the whole show, and ignores or distorts memos from its workforce (the Basic Self) and its employer (the Higher Self). On a good day, it receives *clear, undistorted* messages from the Basic Self ('I feel sad', 'I'm hungry', 'I need to take a walk', 'I feel vulnerable') *and* from the Higher Self ('This is a good moment to phone Tom', 'Here is an opportunity to develop courage and trust') as well as from the outside world. It is quite clear about the *source* of each message, integrates all the information, then takes appropriate action.

Through personal and spiritual growth, the

Conscious Self can become a progressively clearer channel for messages from the Basic Self and Higher Self – and can begin to work in true *partnership* with them.

THE HIGHER SELF

In the Hawaiian language, the Higher Self is known as 'aumakua', which translates as 'utterly trustworthy parental spirit'. It is our mother and father in Spirit – that wise, loving aspect of us which lies beyond fear and doubt, beyond blame and self-pity, beyond negative and limiting beliefs, beyond the illusion of separateness. It is joyful, loving, creative and ever-expanding. In a sense, it is our future self. It is what we are becoming. Our Higher Self loves us unconditionally, never making judgments, never criticising us. It knows why we are here and what we hope to learn – and it guides us on our way Home.

Our Higher Self will never interfere in our lives. This is a planet of free will, and we are here to learn through experience, by making our own decisions. Although our Higher Self might gently nudge us towards our chosen destiny, it never makes a decision *for* us. Fortunately, there are never any 'right' or 'wrong' choices (at a higher level) – simply different choices, with different lessons and opportunities.

The rule is that our Higher Self can help *if it is asked*. So often, we forget to ask! When my friend Mark lost his contact lens in a hotel bedroom, he spent an hour on his hands and knees searching for it, without success. He was going to be late for a meeting. In despair, he briefly closed his eyes and called upon his Higher Self to assist him. The moment he opened his eyes, a glint in the carpet caught his attention. There was the missing lens! His Higher Self had no doubt been waiting patiently for him to call. Another friend asks her Higher Self when the next bus is coming, so that she doesn't have to wait at the bus stop. She reckons she is accurate nine times out of ten.

Every time we ask our Higher Self for help, we are attuning to Spirit – and our Higher Self will jump for joy. There is no limit to how often we can ask our Higher Self (or guides) for help. After all, there is no space-time in their dimension of reality. It isn't as if we might disturb their afternoon tea, or drag them out of bed! Our Higher Self is overjoyed when we become aware of its presence, and delights in offering help and guidance in our everyday lives.

We can also meet our Higher Self in the inner world. In the greater reality, our Higher Self is a conscious energy field; it has no form. However, it can assume a human-like form if we ask to meet it on inner journeys – and you will never discover a more precious friend! My own Higher Self, Cassie, first appeared to me as an angel-like figure of blue light – but after a year or so, she suddenly became much more 'real' and tangible: a tall woman with long, red, curly hair wearing a cloak of deep purple velvet, with her own distinctive 'personality'.

MEETING YOUR HIGHER SELF

Relax deeply, then imagine that you are in a meadow. The grass is lush and green at your feet, and you can see wild flowers – pink, blue and yellow – all around you. The sun is warm against your skin, shining out of a cloudless blue sky. The birds are singing, the air smells sweet, and you feel at peace with yourself. Lying down in the soft grass, you shade your head with a sunhat, and begin to feel drowsy . . .

Asleep in the meadow, you have a strange dream. You dream that you are climbing a huge staircase. The steps seem to go on forever, and you notice there is a pink mist up to your knees. You feel as if you are floating up the steps. Up, up, up you go – until you emerge at the top.

There is a magnificent temple before you. It appears to be built of crystal, and seems almost transparent, though you cannot see inside it. You walk towards the main entrance, then hesitate, wondering whether you are allowed to enter. Suddenly the doors open, as if to welcome you in – and you step inside the massive entrance hall.

No one seems to be there – yet you know that there is someone you must find. You begin to search the temple, room by room. You are looking for your Higher Self. You feel as if you are to meet a long-lost friend. Your heart beats with excitement, with anticipation. And then you wake up . . . and find yourself back in the meadow.

(Repeat this journey until you find your Higher Self in the temple before you 'wake up'. It might happen at the first attempt, or you might need to repeat it several times.)

When you find your Higher Self, start by hugging each other – and ask your Higher Self for its name, so that you can call upon it in your waking life. Then it is time to get to know each other . . . You might wish to tell your Higher Self about your life, your challenges, your Dreams, or to ask about its Dreams for you, or to ask for guidance in following your highest path. Talk to it as you would talk to an intimate friend, learn to hear its gentle voice – and allow yourself to be surprised at what your Higher Self might say or do!

LIVING IN HARMONY

For centuries, spiritual seekers have denied the Basic Self – by denigrating the body, depriving ourselves of food, sleep and physical comfort, or suppressing our feelings, desires and sexuality. The essence of neurosis is inner conflict – yet spiritual traditions, both Eastern and Western, have often encouraged us to battle with ourselves in this way.

The problem is that the Basic Self cannot be 'snipped out' as if it were a malignant tumour. It is part of our wholeness. If we reject our body, emotions or sexuality, we are not being 'spiritual' – we are being neurotic. (Other traditions have suppressed the Conscious Self, instructing its followers to stop thinking, to accept dogma without question, or to meditate until their rational mind wisely gives up!) How can we find our wholeness – our 'holiness' – if we reject any part of ourselves?

An alternative approach is to stop battling, and instead learn to love ourselves. The time for growth through struggle, through separation, through conflict, has passed. It is time now for harmony, for healing, for integration. It is time to recognise that there is nothing 'wrong' with us, nothing within us which is 'bad' or unacceptable – and that our task is to integrate our three selves, to reclaim our wholeness.

According to the Huna wisdom (from Hawaiian shamanism and allied traditions), our three selves are each on their own path of evolution. Our Basic Self will gradually expand its awareness until, in another lifetime, it becomes a Conscious Self. Our Conscious Self is slowly learning how to be a Higher Self. And our Higher Self is becoming an oversoul, on its journey back towards the Source.

This means that a primary task for us (as Conscious Selves) is to become a 'good parent' to our Basic Self, to offer it unconditional love just as our Higher Self does towards us. Even if it seems to be sabotaging our interests, our Basic Self is always doing the best it can. It simply needs our love, help and understanding.

Imagine that our three selves are three carriages of a train. At the front is the Higher Self, in the middle is the Conscious Self, and at the rear is the Basic Self. The Higher Self cannot move any faster unless the Conscious Self comes with it; and the Conscious Self cannot accelerate unless the Basic Self comes too. There has to be harmony between the three selves, each pulling along the self which is 'behind' it, if the train is to move any faster.

We can meditate and pray until we're old and grey – but without our Basic Self, we can never find the wholeness we are seeking. Spirituality cannot be separated from psychology. Unless we deal with our emotional blockages, our childhood patterns, our negative and limiting beliefs, our spiritual growth will always be limited. The Basic Self cannot grow and mature if it is left in the dark. It must be exposed to the Light of awareness and love.

As we learn to nurture our Basic Self – with all its fears and doubts, its resentment and guilt, its neediness and feelings of inadequacy – we expand towards our Higher Self. This is one reason why having children, or caring for animals, can be such a crucial step in our growth. By becoming a loving parent to another, we can learn to love and nurture ourselves.

There is a true story about a very anxious young woman, who had been shivering with fear for several days, and was unable to rise from her bed. Her doctor was very concerned about her, and woke one morning to 'see' a brown rabbit with a white nose hopping over his bed. When his assistant arrived, he asked her to search in the neighbourhood for a rabbit matching this description. She returned an hour later – with the rabbit! The doctor popped the rabbit into his bag, and went to visit his frightened young patient. As he opened his bag, the rabbit hopped on to her bed. 'A look of great tenderness came over her face and from that moment her fear left her.'[2] Her Higher Self had sent her exactly what she needed – a fearful, vulnerable Basic Self to care for – and this had shifted *her* into a higher state.

SELF-LOVE AND SELF-CRITICISM

With a friend or partner: think of a negative message that a parent, teacher or ex-lover used to give you, or which you sometimes give yourself (e.g. 'You never get anything right', 'Your legs are a funny shape', 'You're so selfish', 'You're such a coward'). You don't have to tell your friend what the message is. Now hold an arm up at your side, so that it is parallel to the ground. Repeat the negative message to yourself mentally two or three times, until you can really *feel* it.

Now ask your friend to press down on your arm near to your wrist, using two fingers. Your job is to resist as hard as you can, while keeping the negative message in your mind. You will find – surprise, surprise! – that you have very little strength in your arm. (Any negative message gets straight through to our Basic Self, which believes every word we say.)

Repeat the exercise immediately, using a positive self-message of your choice – it's important to end on a positive note (e.g. 'I love every aspect of myself', 'I am radiant with love and light', 'I am strong and capable'). And notice the huge increase in your strength!

Then swap roles, and let your friend have a go.

(Every thought we have about ourselves – *or about anyone else* – has an instant impact upon our Basic Self. Negative thoughts are disempowering; positive thoughts are empowering.)

THE GIFTS OF THE BASIC SELF

When the Basic Self is loved and nurtured, it has wondrous gifts to offer in return. It fills us with a sense of wonder and aliveness. It gives us child-like spontaneity and playfulness. It makes us charismatic, and fun to be with. It offers good health and vitality. It releases our creativity and inspiration.

The Basic Self is also a stepping stone to our left side. Many young children will speak about past life memories, for instance, since they haven't yet learnt that we are not supposed to *have* past lives! The Basic Self can often do 'the impossible', because it is not restricted by logic and rationality. It can help us to programme the future, release the past, change old habits, heal ourselves and others, develop psychic abilities, receive guidance from our Higher Self, and even work 'miracles'.

Our Higher Self is aware of every request for help, support and guidance – but the rule is that it only *responds* when the Conscious Self and Basic Self are united, so that we learn to integrate our inner selves, and to heal our inner Child.

Similarly, messages from our Higher Self come *via* the Basic Self. Most of my own intuitive flashes come not from speaking *directly* with my guides or Higher Self, but rather as bodily knowing, a twinge in my gut as a thought or idea comes to me, or as visual images, 'snapshots' of the future, accompanied by a rush of excitement or enthusiasm. In other words, these messages come *via* the Basic Self – via the body and physical sensations. Unless we are attuned with our Basic Self, it is difficult to receive higher guidance.

On the other hand, we need to be clear about the difference between guidance from our Higher Self and impulses from our subconscious mind. Linda grew up with unhappily married parents who were barely civil to each other, and her father worked in the same dreary office for forty years. As an adult, not surprisingly, Linda was afraid of commitment, seeing it as a form of imprisonment. After a year or two in any job, home or relationship, Linda would cut-and-run. She kidded herself that she was 'following her heart' in walking out if a situation was less than perfect or when the going got tough. She scuttled from one experience to the next, always splashing about in the shallow end of life. Others saw her as strong, independent and decisive; but the reality was that she was stuck in a compulsive pattern – running away from commitment and intimacy, in response to impulses from her fearful Basic Self.

So how can we tell the difference? How can we know whether an impulse is higher guidance, or comes from our wounded inner Child? The answer is that there is no universal, foolproof test! This is all part of the fun and challenge of being alive. Each of us has to learn through self-awareness and personal experience. However – as a general guide – acting upon a subconscious impulse often gives an immediate sense of relief, followed by a gradual build-up of the same old uneasiness. It often comes with a 'hurried' or compulsive quality, and an inability to think clearly. It might be accompanied by anxiety, tension, sleepiness, fatigue, or a sense of 'closing down' and becoming smaller. Higher guidance tends to have a more open, relaxed quality. It seems to expand our sense of self, and might feel scary but exciting.

Of course, even if an impulse *is* bubbling up from our subconscious, it should still be taken seriously – though not necessarily *acted upon*. After all, it is a gift from our Basic Self, revealing unmet needs or desires, suppressed emotions, fears or emotional patterns which need to be understood and healed. Everything that comes to us is our friend.

BEFRIENDING OUR BASIC SELF

The first essential, if we are to harmonise our inner selves, is to befriend our Basic Self. Once it feels loved and respected, the Basic Self is usually eager to learn and grow – but we need to speak its language, as we would with a small child.

There are seven principles to bear in mind:

1. Motivation
The Basic Self is motivated by a need for survival and security, and a desire for pleasure. Whatever you wish to create or change, think of reasons which will appeal to your Basic Self. If you want to sell your house, your Basic Self might be scared, because it remembers moving house when you were small, and how insecure and lonely it felt. You might need to reassure it that you, the Conscious Self, will always be there, that it will not be alone – and remind it of all the reasons why moving house would be pleasurable and exciting.

If you want to meditate regularly, it's no use talking to your Basic Self about 'enlightenment' – it's much too abstract a goal. However, it might like the idea of being more creative, more focused, more relaxed, working with unseen friends or exploring other dimensions of reality. Or perhaps you could promise yourself a gift or holiday if you meditate at least four times a week. Forget about being 'spiritual' – you need to get your Inner Child motivated!

Ask your Basic Self whether it has any fears or doubts about changes you want to make. You can meet it on an inner journey. Or you might ask 'How do you feel about moving house/meditating regularly?' – either mentally, or out loud – while holding a pen and notepad. *Using your non-dominant hand* (i.e. the left hand if you're right-handed, and vice versa), write down whatever comes to mind. Keep offering good reasons for making the change, or reassurance that its old fears are no longer appropriate, until your Basic Self seems willing to give it a go.

2. Emotion

A telltale sign that the Basic Self is not in harmony is when we ask for help, guidance, healing, success or an opportunity, and yet don't *feel* anything. Without the Basic Self, we feel rather 'dead', cerebral, just going through the motions. If we pray or use an affirmation from our Conscious Self alone, we're wasting our time; we might as well recite a shopping list. When the Basic Self is involved, any request is 'heartfelt'. There is a feeling of love, desire, enthusiasm, excitement, energy and power – particularly around the heart and solar plexus. (The solar plexus is the centre of the Basic Self. The heart symbolises the 'meeting place' between the Basic Self and Conscious Self.)

3. Imagery

The Basic Self 'thinks' mostly in images and symbols, rather than words. Unlike the Conscious Self, it doesn't distinguish between real and imaginary – it treats whatever it experiences as 'real'. The joy of this is that we can rehearse any situation in our minds, seeing the outcome that we desire, and our Basic Self will believe it has already happened. The more vividly we imagine it, the more strongly our Basic Self gets the message. If you visualise yourself succeeding – winning a race, finishing your novel, creating a fine sculpture, being offered a promotion, clinching a business deal – then your Basic Self believes you have already done it, and will do whatever is necessary to 'repeat' the success in reality.

The Basic Self doesn't distinguish between past, present and future. It lives in the eternal Now. The *disadvantage* of this is that a vivid memory from the past, highly charged with emotion, can still create problems, ten, twenty or fifty years later, as if it only happened yesterday. However, the *advantage* is that we can heal the past – just as we can programme the future – by vividly imagining it.

A friend once phoned to ask me about a brief but puzzling dream. In the dream, she was in a house she had lived in many years before. The hall was lined with walk-in cupboards, and one of these doors slowly opened to reveal a skeleton. Since the dream was clearly a message about a 'skeleton in her cupboard', I suggested that she re-enter it as a waking dream, and ask the skeleton some questions. The next day, she phoned in some excitement to tell me what had happened. The skeleton had appeared on cue, and she had asked what it was trying to tell her. No response. So she kept it simple. 'Is it something that happened while I was living in this house?' The skeleton shook its head vigorously. 'Is it something that happened when I was a child?' The skeleton nodded. 'How old was I?' No response. The skeleton would only answer Yes – No questions. 'Was I three years old? Four? Five? Six?' The skeleton nodded at six. A sudden inspiration hit her, as she recalled an incident she had forgotten for twenty years or more. 'Was it when that neighbour touched me in the back of the car?' Yes, yes, yes! The skeleton became very excited, and began to dance! So that was the problem – but how was she to resolve it? 'Should I go back and change this memory?' The skeleton nodded again, and danced back into the cupboard. Its job was complete. My friend vividly imagined the childhood event, and saw herself getting out of the car without having been molested – and the memory was healed.

4. Deep breathing and relaxation

Whenever we relax, we shift our awareness from the narrow focus of the Conscious Self, and make space for the Basic Self (and Higher Self) to 'speak' to us – through emotions, images, sensations, intuitive flashes, words or memories. Anything which encourages us to relax and breathe deeply – dancing, gardening, walking in nature, inner journeys, yoga – helps us stay in touch with our Basic Self.

Relaxation and breathing also help us to speak to our Higher Self. The Hawaiians refer to foreigners as 'haoles', which means 'without breath', because they observed that Christian missionaries prayed *without* first building up mana (power) by breathing deeply. Prayers 'without breath', according to the Hawaiians, will not be effective, since prayers must carry 'power' from our Basic Self.

5. Repetition

The Basic Self is a slow learner, and needs plenty of repetition. Affirmations can work 'miracles', but only if we use them persistently and regularly, until our Basic Self finally gets the message. Since it is a creature of habit, the Basic Self tends to resist change at first – but once a new habit is established, it usually sticks.

The Conscious Self is quick to learn, but its learning is often confined to the intellectual level. If your Conscious Self alone is reading this book, you will read it quickly, intending to come back to the exercises later – then you'll place it back on the bookshelf and move on to the *next* book, failing to integrate the knowledge into your daily life. Your Basic Self, on the other hand, would read much more slowly and carefully, choosing exercises which feel exciting, eagerly wanting to *experience* what the book is all about. Slowly but surely, it *absorbs* what is said, and can put it into practice. If your Conscious Self and your Basic Self read the book together, then your 'knowledge' has a good chance of becoming 'wisdom' – that is, knowledge that you *live*.

Since it is child-like, the Basic Self is also impressed by authority – so it can be wise to read books or go to lectures which 'confirm' what we already know, to reassure our Basic Self that our ideas are not so crazy after all!

6. Action and ritual

The Basic Self is much more impressed by actions than by thoughts. If you just *think* about writing a novel, the Basic Self will probably ignore you; but if you buy a special notebook or computer disk, and start jotting down plots and characters, it will become more interested, and begin to send you inspiration. If you *think* about wanting to release a former relationship, the Basic Self might just yawn, since it's heard it all before; but if you throw out your old photos and memorabilia, and complete a 'fire ceremony' (see Chapter 4), it will know that you mean business – and will throw up any unresolved emotions which you need to deal with, so that you can finally let go.

By using our physical body, by taking action, we build a bridge between the inner and outer worlds – and open ourselves to change. Whatever you wish to do, it is crucial to take action – however small, however symbolic – to tell your Basic Self that you're serious about it.

For the same reason, it is important to write down or speak about an inner journey, since this action brings it into the outer world. (Similarly, it is more powerful to pray out loud, or to write down a request to Spirit, rather than to pray silently.) Even better, re-create an inner journey in the physical world in some way. If your Higher Self gives you a peacock feather, find a 'real' peacock feather – or perhaps draw or paint it. If you walked along a cliff-top in the inner world, as a symbol of gaining higher perspective on your life, then find a 'real' clifftop to walk along.

The Basic Self is impressed by anything which

creates a strong sensory impression: light, colour, music, scent, drumming, singing, costumes, dance, movement ... If you create a ceremony or ritual, with plenty of sensory input, to mark a transition in your life, your Basic Self will know that something important has happened, and do whatever is needed to help you make the shift. (For example, the *Conscious Self* might see getting married as rather silly and unnecessary, as an 'empty ritual'; whereas for the *Basic Self*, a wedding can be a crucial rite of passage, a richly symbolic act of love and commitment which it takes very seriously.)

Whenever we decide to change our lives, it is the Basic Self which needs to be engaged. So if you need to take a 'leap of faith', why not jump off a fence, or boulder – just high enough to scare you a little, but not high enough to risk injury – with the clear *focus* and *intent* that this leap is symbolic of the 'real' leap of faith which you will soon take in your life. Or if you wish to release a burden – such as guilt, martyrhood, or a job you dislike – carry a heavy weight on your back. Walk around the room *feeling* the burden, until you are more than ready to drop it – then let go.[3]

When your Basic Self feels the sense of freedom and excitement that comes from completing such a ritual, it will alleviate its fear of change. Rituals can be amazingly powerful!

7. Living with joy

When we live in harmony with our Basic Self, our days will include plenty of fun – perhaps dancing, singing, walking in the woods, eating out, meeting friends, making love, travelling, sketching, painting, shopping, sleeping late, watching the sun rise, going to the movies, sailing, rollerskating, playing with children, writing poetry, walking the dog, picnicking, hang-gliding, skinnydipping, sitting in coffee shops . . .

What is more, we will take every opportunity to *celebrate*: birthdays, anniversaries, festivals, successes, arrivals, departures, full and new moons, equinoxes and solstices – and simply celebration of life itself!

It's worth asking what 'fun' and 'celebration' mean to you, and whether you are living with joy. If not, you are not being a good-enough parent to your Basic Self. You are confirming its belief that it doesn't deserve to have fun, that life is hard work, that fun is an occasional treat which must be 'earned'. You are rubbing salt into its wounds – and reinforcing a pattern of growth through struggle.

Living with joy is an essential aspect of honouring our Basic Self. As we create more and more joy in our lives, our Basic Self begins to feel worthy and deserving. Its fears and doubts diminish, the child-hood wounds begin to heal – and its wondrous gifts begin to unfold.

4

Dancing Your Dream Awake

'I could tell you my adventures – beginning from this morning,' said Alice, a little timidly, 'but it's no use going back to yesterday because I was a different person then.'
(Lewis Carroll[1])

When Alice disappeared down the rabbit hole, she had one goal in mind: she wanted to chase the White Rabbit. While searching for him, she was forced to question all of her basic assumptions about reality – and to develop her courage, compassion and humility. She also had a great deal of fun! Her goal was unimportant; it was the journey that mattered. Alice's desire to find the White Rabbit was just an excuse for her adventures in Wonderland.

Everyone needs a White Rabbit. Everyone needs to have Dreams which inspire us to reach for the stars, to push through our fears, to explore our potential, to become more of who we are. When we chase our Dreams, we are forever growing and changing, simply because our desire motivates us to keep moving on.

What if Alice had hesitated at the top of the rabbit hole, wondering whether chasing the White Rabbit was silly, or impossible? Or whether there was something more important, more worthy, she should do?

Or whether someone else might be *better* at chasing White Rabbits? Or whether she was being too unconventional, and should take up sewing instead? Or whether she should just be satisfied with life, and forget all about the White Rabbit? If so, Alice would be forgotten by now – and what an adventure she would have missed! Yet how often do we give ourselves similar excuses for not following our Dreams?

I recently saw an inspiring TV documentary about a young man who had given up his 'sensible' job, sold his house, bought a mobile library to live in – and had become a monster hunter at Loch Ness. People sometimes asked him whether he was mad. As he pointed out, such people were often working in dull 9-to-5 jobs, just to support their leisure time – whereas he was living on the shores of a beautiful Scottish loch, spending every day doing what he had always dreamt of doing. Who was really mad? His closing words were: 'If you don't follow your Dreams, the only loser is you.'

We are here to learn, grow and have fun – life is an adventure in consciousness – and our White Rabbits offer an exciting path into the future. By following our hearts, by following our bliss, we are choosing growth through joy. There will be many challenges along the way – from Mad Hatters to Mock Turtles – but we can see every event as an opportunity, as a part of our chosen adventure.

If we ignore our White Rabbits, pretend we haven't seen them, or agonise over which rabbit hole to run down, we might *believe* that we are 'playing safe' – but in fact, the opposite is true. Our Higher Self, which loves us unconditionally, yearns for us to learn and grow – and if we refuse to grow through joy, it will reluctantly send us struggle. Illness, suffering, emotional trauma, accidents and injury are all kicks to grow; if we ignore the 'carrot' of our Dreams, then we invite the 'stick' of struggle.

Of course, this doesn't mean that we all have to be wildly adventurous. White Rabbits come in many different forms – from setting up a business to bringing up a child, from committing yourself to a relationship to running a marathon. All that matters is having a Dream, and throwing one's heart and soul into moving towards it. Some people, like Alice, have one White Rabbit which guides much of their life's journey. Others have a whole warren of rabbits, leading us down many different holes. It doesn't matter – all that matters is having a Dream.

CIRCLE OF DREAMS

Draw a circle on a large sheet of paper, so that the circle almost fills the page. Inside the circle, write down your own White Rabbits: everything that you want to do, have or learn in the next five to ten years. For example: country cottage, saxophone, computer, learn about aromatherapy, go on safari, learn to play didgeridoo, get married, travel to China, make close friends, creative work, set up own business, write a science-fiction novel, grow vegetables, swim in a coral reef, learn about wild flowers . . . Or perhaps you just have one big Dream, something which has lurked in the back of your mind for years, a Dream which you scarcely dare to own as a possibility? If so, write it in huge capital letters.

Around the edge of the circle, write down your *global* Dreams. How do you wish to see the world change in the next five to ten years? What matters most to you?

Attune to Spirit before you begin, and allow yourself to be surprised by what comes to mind. Make sure that you write down what you really want, not what you think you *should* want, or what you *used* to want. Your true Dreams will make you feel excited. Think big! Think limitlessly!

(I always use circles for this exercise because we learn to write from left to right, from top to bottom; that is, we write from our right side, which thinks in a rational, linear way. When we write in a circle, filling it higgledy-piggledy or in a spiral, we're more likely to tap into our left side, our intuition. Notice whether, despite writing in a circle, you still tend to write in neat little lines!)

This is not a one-off exercise, since our Dreams are forever growing and changing. I suggest preparing a Circle of Dreams *at least* twice a year.

Ask, and it shall be given you;
seek, and ye shall find;
knock, and it shall be opened unto you;
For everyone that asketh receiveth;
and he that seeketh findeth;
and to him that knocketh it shall be opened.
                            (Matthew 7: 7–8)

Twenty years ago, when I was still at school, this passage from the Bible 'happened' to be the one I read in front of the school assembly. As I read, I expanded to fill the huge hall, and became aware of the playing fields, the nearby sand-dunes and the sea beyond. I considered myself Buddhist at that time, yet these verses had always had a profound impact on me.

I pondered the meaning of this passage for many years, convinced that it held a mystical secret of the universe. It was obvious that people do *not* always get what they ask for, that prayers are *not* always answered. Yet it did seem that, on the whole, people's *expectations* were fulfilled. Those who always feared the worst, and dwelt on possible disasters, seemed to attract 'bad luck'; while those who were optimistic appeared to be more 'fortunate'.

It wasn't until I came across the Seth books,[2] in my early twenties, that I began to understand. We create our own reality. Every thought is a prayer. 'Ask and it shall be given you.' Every thought, every belief, every desire, every fear, every expectation, is a form of 'asking', and magnetises the corresponding reality.

An American friend of mine went to live in central London, and bought a car. However, the heavy traffic and restricted parking soon made her regret her decision. 'I wish I didn't have that car,' she thought to herself. No sooner said than done. The car was stolen, and she never saw it again!

When I bought my first flat near Liverpool, I was full of negative beliefs about the area, about my finances, and about purpose-built flats. As a result, it took several years to sell the property, and I lost thousands of pounds – despite a property boom. The flat was even burgled!

By the time I sold my next house, I no longer just *believed* that we create our own reality, I *knew* it. I was not going to repeat my old mistakes. By now, the housing market was in the grip of a recession, prices were plummeting, and little was selling. However, I was quite determined. I processed my motives and beliefs, used a 'cone of power' technique,[3] then phoned the estate agents. Within a week, the house was sold – at a handsome profit.

Desires have had a very bad press on the spiritual path – but how can we create a heaven on Earth without desires? It is desire which motivates us to change the world, to fulfil our potential, to form loving relationships, to become all that we can be. Enthusiasm comes from 'en theos', meaning 'the God within'. Any desire which comes from the heart is a message from our Higher Self – a White Rabbit which will lead us where we need to go.

Does God/dess really *want* us to have fun? Aren't we supposed to be terribly serious, pray and meditate all day, repent our sins, and humbly beg for forgiveness? No, no, no! If *you* had bestowed the gift of life to conscious beings, would you want them to cherish that gift, to revel in their adventure, to bubble with laughter and joy; or would you want them to say, with a martyred sigh, 'This is a terrible place to be, and I'm probably being punished. But perhaps I'll get to heaven if I suffer enough?' God/dess is boundless love, joy and creativity – why should S/He want us to be miserable?

'But isn't it selfish and greedy to want a lovely home or a new car, when so many people are starving or homeless?' Such a question assumes that the world is a fixed, solid reality. But life is a dream that we are creating, a three-dimensional illusion. If you suddenly became aware that you were asleep and dreaming, would you say to yourself, 'Well, I'd better not create too big a house in this dream. After all, some people don't have a house at all'? Or would you say, 'Hey, I'm dreaming! Let's have some fun! How about creating a beautiful house with sweeping lawns and a fountain'? The world is only limited by our beliefs – and as we drop our own limitations, others can be inspired to drop theirs. As we learn how to create our Dreams, we can help others to do so. We do not help anyone by limiting ourselves.

As Bartholomew[4] puts it,

> *If you say looking for money is separate from looking for God, you may never have either . . . God is the yearning to have an empowered way of being in the world so that one feels one is doing what one wants to do. That is God in action. God sells books. God runs a computer. God teaches. God learns. God loves children. God creates beauty. God drives a truck. God helps others. God is. Don't separate . . . Whatever you yearn for, whatever face it is taking, it is God.*

The only risk from chasing our Dreams is that we might kid ourselves that we won't be happy until we 'get there'. The whole point is our journey, not our destination. We are not living on Earth *in order* to get somewhere else; we are here to enjoy the adventure of being here! Whatever our Dreams, we have to remember that the process *is* the goal.

If you have convinced yourself that 'I'll be happy when I resign from this job/get married/finish my novel/have a new washing machine/get my degree/have a child/next week . . .', then you have forgotten that this moment, *right now*, is the time to be happy. Unless we can dance our Dreams awake, when will we ever dance at all?

CREATING WHAT WE WANT

Whatever we wish to create in our lives – success at work, more free time, a new career, peace of mind, selling a house, opportunities to travel, becoming a parent, winning a lottery, or finding a life partner – there is a nine-step process to go through. If you're serious about your Dream, don't just *think about* the nine steps. Keep a journal of each step, and enjoy the process of *learning how* to create what you want.

Step 1: Clarify what you want
Listen to your heart, and be specific about what you want. For example, if you want a loving relationship, what qualities are you seeking in that relationship, or in the other person? If you want a new car, what would its qualities be? (Perhaps being reliable, comfort-able, attractive to look at, quiet, economical, using lead-free petrol – or whatever? Perhaps you want a specific make or colour?) Clarifying what you want is an essential first step in getting your energy focused.

For Steps 1 and 2, I use what I call 'spider charts' – a small central circle, with lines drawn from it like the legs of a spider. (See page 66.) Inside the first circle, you could write 'What I want'. At the end of each spider's leg, write down any details or qualities which come to mind.

Bear in mind that your Higher Self is much more concerned with essence than with form. Focusing on qualities – on the *essence* of what you want – gives your Higher Self the option of creating a *form* you might not have considered. For example, you might wish to get married, but if you clarify what you really want from a relationship – perhaps companionship, affection, laughter, sharing, independence, shared expenses – you might find that sharing a house with close friends would suit you even better.

On the other hand, I'm often very specific about details (while being open to other possibilities). Before moving to Dorset, I prepared a long list of 'essentials' for my new house: character cottage at least two hundred years old, two large reception rooms, oak beams, open fireplaces, south-facing garden, in one of two villages – and so on. When I went to look for a house, I just made one phone call, and the first property I was offered was my ideal home. Programming can save a lot of wasted time!

Next, write down *why* you want it. (You could draw another spider chart for this.) How will it help you to learn and grow, or fulfil more of your potential, or help you to enjoy life? It's perfectly OK to want something because it would be fun – so long as it's what would be fun *for you*. Learning how to create what we want is an opportunity to discover what we *really* want, as opposed to what 'most people' want, or what we used to want, or what our family expects of us, or what fits an image we wish to project. It's much easier to create a Dream which really comes from your heart.

Whatever our heart desires is 'spiritual' in essence – whether it is a pot plant or a washing machine. At one workshop, a man asked whether it was OK to try to manifest a sports car. When I asked him what a sports car symbolised for him, he said freedom, empowerment, independence, prosperity and fun. In other words, a sports car was an outer *symbol* of those inner qualities. So couldn't he develop those qualities *without* having a sports car? Yes, of course – but we are here to *engage* with the material world not to retreat from it, and we have to realise that physical reality is always an outer symbol of our inner world. The point is to *learn how* to create what we want – and not to take the 'form' too seriously!

It is important to be *clear* and *consistent* about what we want. So often, we fail to create something because we are unsure what we want, keep changing our minds, or feel uneasy about asking. At one workshop with Emmanuel (channelled by Pat Rodegast), I remember a woman who had been declared infertile asking whether she should simply *accept* that she wasn't meant to have children. In his reply (which wouldn't apply to *every* 'infertile' woman) Emmanuel told her that sometimes we need to 'develop our lung capacity' in shouting persistently for what we want – and that this can be a crucial lesson in itself. (He added that he could 'see' two little souls packing their suitcases!)

Similarly, I have often seen clients who say that they long for a committed relationship, yet repeatedly have affairs with married men or long-distance lovers. They are unclear about what they really want. Since we create our own reality, the truth is that such people 'really' want romance and physical intimacy

Processing: examples of spider charts

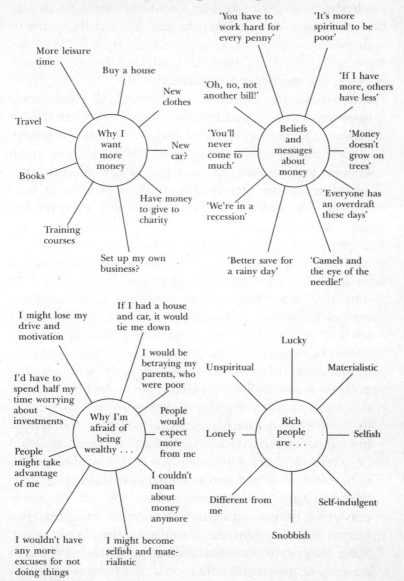

without day-to-day commitment (or 'really' want to experience strong emotions, or 'really' want frustration) – at least for the time being. When we 'really' want a committed relationship, there it is!

Step 2: Examine your beliefs

Let's suppose that you want to create X. The next step is to process your beliefs and attitudes. Create another spider chart, and write in the circle: 'My beliefs about X' – include thoughts that run through your head, what your parents used to say, any memories that come to mind, and messages your hear from friends or in the media, as well as the beliefs which you 'own' as yours. Allow yourself to be surprised – and resist the temptation to 'censor' thoughts which you would like to disown! The Basic Self often clings to beliefs long after the Conscious Self has discarded them.

The next step is to look at your resistance. We always get what we want, so if you are not creating X, you must be blocking it. You need to clarify what stands in the way: negative beliefs or attitudes, fears and doubts, anger and resentment, guilt, feeling undeserving, or payoffs such as self-pity, punishing others, feeling better than others or avoiding responsibility.

In your next spider chart, write in the circle: 'Why I can't have X' or 'What might stop me having X'. At the end of each spider leg, write down whatever comes to mind (e.g. I can't afford it; I don't deserve it; Relationships never work out for me; We're in a recession; I haven't got time; My childhood messed me up; I'm too old/young; I'm not talented enough; I have too many responsibilities). What are the excuses you give yourself?

Now prepare another spider chart, and write in the circle: 'I'm afraid that if I get X . . .'. Again, draw lines coming out from the circle, and at the end of each line, write down whatever comes to mind. Allow yourself to be surprised by the thoughts that come up. This is a good way of tapping into any fears that might be blocking you. (Another useful spider chart here is: 'It's better not to have X because . . .' or 'The good thing about my current situation is . . .'. For example: It feels safe; I can feel sorry for myself; I get help from others; I have lots of time alone.)

Now one more spider chart: 'People who have X are . . .'. On this chart, write down any thoughts about people who have a soul-mate, or a new car, or the kind of job you want. We often have negative beliefs about 'those kind of people', or see ourselves as different from them in some way – perhaps seeing them as self-absorbed, or workaholic, or boring, or more intelligent, or more outgoing – which blocks us from getting what we want.

If you wish, make up your own additional spider charts. Steps 1 and 2 should take less than half an hour. By this time, *if you have been honest with yourself*, you should have a good idea of how and why you are blocking what you want.

Step 3: Transform your inner blockages

When you filled in your Circle of Dreams, you might have noticed an inner voice criticising or objecting to your Dreams, or little tugs of resistance in your solar plexus. Since everything is our friend, I always assume that these inner blockages are trying to help in some way. More often than not, they are aspects of the Basic Self which are trying to 'stay safe', or feel undeserving, or are striving to fulfil outdated scripts and contracts. (Since the Basic Self carries our memories of other lifetimes, the blockages might even come from traumatic experiences or vows taken in other lifetimes.) Once acknowledged and updated, these blockages are usually more than willing to help, and this step can be enormous fun.

You can use the inner journey in Chapter 2, *Meeting the Struggler*, to meet and transform your own inner blockages, or you can work directly with your Basic Self. I usually meet my inner Child too, to check out how she feels about my Dreams. (Beware of a little voice telling you that you can miss out this step, since you have already cleared your blockages! It's trying to fool you!)

When I decided to attract a soul-mate, I took an inner journey to meet any blockages. I was shown into a small office, and greeted by a dark-haired secretary with thick-rimmed glasses. When I informed her of my purpose, she took an index card file, thumbed through it expertly, and removed four cards – two of which were well-thumbed and tattered. She explained the objections listed on each card, and said that the complainants were willing to meet me. It was all very business-like.

The first objectors were an array of nuns, monks, priests, yogis and hermits, all of whom claimed that I had taken vows of celibacy! I had to convince each of them of the spiritual growth which could be gained from love, intimacy and commitment, and about the importance of spiritualising sexuality. I also reminded them that, in *this* lifetime, I had not agreed to be celibate! Another objector was my creative muse, who warned me that I was always less creative and productive while involved in a relationship. I promised to change this belief, and asked for the muse's help in finding a partner who would stimulate and support my creativity. And so it went on . . .

Alternatively – or in addition – you can focus on changing any negative thoughts or beliefs. A good way to start is by using affirmations – positive statements which affirm that what you want is coming into your life, or which state the reverse of any limiting beliefs or fears. (Look back at your spider charts, or remember what your inner blockages told you, to see what you need to change.) For example:

- I am now attracting a soul-mate.
- The perfect job is now coming into my life.
- The more money I have, the more I can give.
- Whatever I truly desire, I can have.
- It is the perfect time to sell my house.
- My relationships are now loving and supportive. And so on.

Affirmations should be brief and to the point. If you use long, wordy affirmations, your Basic Self will just fall asleep. Also, it's important to write down an affirmation, or speak it out loud. It won't have as much impact if you just think it. (You could write it on small cards for your fridge, mirror, desk, radio – wherever you'll often see it.) Repeat it to yourself, *with feeling*, as often as you remember.

If you say an affirmation while walking on the spot, slapping each hand to the opposite knee as it rises, it 'locks' the affirmation into both sides of the brain (according to applied kinesiology). It also makes you feel very silly, which probably makes it more memorable to the Basic Self! It seems to work.

Of course, it's no good using affirmations for ten minutes each day if you're full of fears and doubts during the rest of the day. It's what we think 24 hours a day that really counts. Every thought is a prayer. Every thought-form is energy which goes out into the universe on our behalf. Affirmations only work when we use them to change our thinking.

If an affirmation seems like a 'lie' at first, it is only because we're identifying with a limited, negative aspect of ourselves. Using an affirmation helps us to resonate with that part of us which already 'knows' that the affirmation is true. Once we make that shift, the affirmation begins to seem obvious and super-fluous – and the work is done.

If you hear a fear or doubt run through your mind, it is important not to criticise or judge yourself, or try to suppress it. The thought is bubbling up from your Basic Self to be healed. So *welcome* the thought ('Hello, I hear you!'), send love and reassurance to that frightened or cynical part of yourself, say that you now release the thought, and gently replace it with your affirmation. Similarly, if someone else expresses fears and doubts, remind yourself that they are reflecting back your own fear and doubt – and deal with it in the same way.

Step 4: Ask for unseen help
By this stage, you are clear about what you want and why, and have cleared any inner blockages. Now is

the time to ask your Higher Self, guides or any other unseen friends for help (see Chapter 7). Attune to Spirit, then mentally ask for what you want – or meet your unseen friends on an inner journey. If you feel any resistance to asking your Higher Self for what you want, then maybe the desire is not coming from your heart, or perhaps your Basic Self is holding on to guilt, or to limiting beliefs. Either way, you need to retrace your steps until you can freely and joyfully ask for what you want.

Sometimes all we need to do is ask. When I flew to Honolulu, I put in a request to Spirit that I would find a 'talking stick' in Hawaii. (A talking stick is passed around the circle in a group or workshop, giving its holder the right to speak without being interrupted.) I wanted a 'female' talking stick – curved, gnarled and comfortable to hold.

I combed the Hawaiian beaches for a week or so without any luck. Then one afternoon, I strolled past the beach hut where we slept at night – and stopped in astonishment. Lying on the bottom step of the hut, as if carefully placed there by hand, was a beautiful 'talking stick'. (I had not mentioned to anyone that I was searching for a talking stick, and had seen nothing remotely similar in Hawaii.) 'Ask, and it shall be given you.' I gave thanks to Spirit, and have used the talking stick in workshops ever since. Many people have commented on its powerful energy.

Step 5: Programme what you want
Desire, imagination and expectancy pull our Dreams towards us. These are the magnets which help us create what we want. Start by choosing an image

which sums up your Dream. If it's a new job, it might be an image of you in your new office; if it's a loving relationship, it might be walking along a beach hand-in-hand, or cooking an evening meal together; if you want more energy and vitality, your image might be leaping out of bed at dawn, or dancing until the small hours . . . Or you might have a whole series of images, either moving or still.

As often as you like, *visualise* what you want, and involve all of your senses – *hear* the clatter of word processors, *smell* the food cooking, *taste* the sea air on your lips, *feel* your lover's hand in yours. Make it real. At the same time, conjure up strong emotions of joy and desire. Feel your enthusiasm. This ensures that your Basic Self is in harmony with your Conscious Self, that you're not just 'going through the motions'. Emotions act rather like an accelerator pedal – the stronger the emotion, the more rapidly you attract what you want.

Just one word of warning – your desire must fall short of desperation. If you believe that you cannot survive without X, your Higher Self is quite likely to say, 'Oh yes, you can!' and block it coming to you – because it wants you to know that your happiness does *not* depend on having a new job, or more money, or an intimate relationship. Desperation usually *repels* what we want. Our desires should be centred in our heart, not in the need for survival. It's far easier to manifest a Dream if our attitude is 'I really, really want this – but if I don't get it, it's OK. I can be happy without it.'

Don't forget the expectancy! I often use the analogy of switching on a light. When we turn on a light, we *expect* the room to be flooded with light. We don't hesitate over the switch, thinking to ourselves, 'Oh,

I *do* hope this light works. I do *want* it to work!' –
we just *expect* it to work. Almost invariably, it does!
Yet when we programme our Dreams, we often lose
this faith and trust, and resort to 'hoping' instead.
Hope is a much weaker magnet than expectancy.

Step 5 can also involve rituals – such as lighting a
candle for your Dream. The Basic Self likes ritual and
ceremony. I sometimes hold a candle while programming what I want, so that the candle picks up the energy.
(I use green candles for prosperity, pink for love and
healing, white or yellow for creativity and inspiration –
but use whatever colour feels right to you.) Then I light
the candle while affirming that, as it burns down, energy
will go out into the universe and attract what I am
asking for, or something even better. I always ask for
help from Spirit in creating my Dream – 'in the service
of All Our Relations' or 'in the name of love and light'.

If you perform a ritual, attune to Spirit and treat
it as a sacred act – but also keep a sense of lightness
and fun. Don't worry about whether you are 'getting
it right'. As long as your heart is in what you are
doing, you are getting it right!

(Incidentally, you can also ask other people to 'hold
a vision' for you, to help co-create what you want.
Just tell them exactly what you want, and ask them
to desire, imagine and expect it for you – and/or do
the same for others.)

Step 6: Release the past

Every birth means dying to our past. Whenever we
make a change in our lives, we have to release our
old beliefs, emotional patterns, lifestyle and/or self-
image – and even when the change is positive, we

need to grieve for what has gone before. (Many women who suffer from post-natal depression, for example, are grieving for their loss of freedom and independence, the loss of their former self. Getting married, divorced or starting a new job, similarly, is often followed by feeling depressed for a while. Depression is often a natural response to a sudden change in lifestyle – a form of grieving.)

It helps to be clear about exactly *what* you are giving up, and to make a conscious decision to let go of the past. Whatever you are trying to manifest, make a list of what you will need to release. Then assess whether the likely advantages will outweigh the likely costs – or whether you are prepared to follow your heart, whatever the consequences. If so, then allow yourself to feel your sadness about leaving behind this stage in your life. (A few years ago, when I was guided to move to London, I realised that I'd have to sell my much-loved home in Devon. One day, I sat down at the top of the stairs, and sobbed and sobbed! But I knew that I was making the right decision.) If we block grief and other emotions, it can prevent us from moving on, or creating what we want, since our energy is still 'leaking out' to the past.

If you are releasing an *unpleasant* situation – such as a job you dislike, an abusive marriage, or living in a tiny, damp bedsit – it is crucial to clarify what you have learnt from the experience. Give thanks for the lessons learnt, or the strengths and personal qualities you have developed, so that you can walk away with good grace. (Bitterness, guilt and resentment always tie us to the past, which means that we will recreate a similar situation in the future.)

RELEASING THE PAST

(The ideal time for this fire ceremony is during the dark of the moon, or during an equinox or solstice, but it can be used at any time. It comes from the Native American traditions.)

1. Clarify what you wish to release – perhaps a relationship, a house, a childhood pattern, your martyrhood, blocked-up grief, or perhaps releasing a future you had once envisioned, before your life took an unexpected direction. (It might help to attune to Spirit and ask 'What do I need to release?' – then wait and listen.) Also clarify what you wish to 'give birth to' – the future which you want to create.

2. Gather together a candle, one or two pieces of paper and a pen, a fireproof pot – I keep a casserole specifically for this purpose – and symbol(s) of whatever you wish to release, such as a photograph of the person, an old school tie, a house key, a green scarf for jealousy, or salt water for grief. Use your imagination. If you have an object which is already 'charged' with the energy of that person, situation or emotion, so much the better. If you are not willing to burn the object(s), or if it will not burn, then write down what you wish to release on a piece of paper. On a separate piece of paper, write down what you wish to create.

3. Place the candle next to the fireproof pot, on a small table or altar, or on the floor. You might also wish to set the

atmosphere with music, incense or oils.
(Traditionally one should face the East, the
place of the rising sun, for this ceremony.)
Light the candle, then attune to Spirit.

4. Call upon Spirit using whatever words
come to you. For example, 'I call upon the
spirits of the four directions to be with me
now: the spirits of the East, the West, the
South and North. I call upon my guides and
other unseen friends. I call upon the Great
Spirit, Wakan-Tanka, All That Is, to help me
in releasing the past and giving birth to the
future.' Or more simply, 'Spirit, please be with
me for this ceremony of release.'

5. Now take one of the symbols you wish to
release, and talk from your heart to Spirit
(out loud if possible) about what the symbol
represents, what you have learnt from it, and
why you are ready to release it. Then use the
candle to set light to the object (or piece of
paper), and burn it in the fireproof pot.

Call upon the fire to release and transform
the symbols. 'I call upon the Spirit of Fire, and
all of my unseen friends, to help me in
releasing the past. I have learnt the lessons, I
have become more of who I am, and I am
ready to move on. Please help me in freeing
myself from the past, so that I can walk into
the future with love and joy, hand in hand with
Spirit.' (Use whatever words feel appropriate.)

Repeat with each symbol in turn.

6. By releasing the past, you have now created a vacuum, so quickly fill it with your vision of the future. Take the piece of paper which holds your Dream for the future, tell Spirit what you wish to create, ask for unseen help – and burn the paper in the fireproof pot.

7. Give thanks to Spirit, and blow out the candle.

RELEASING THE PAST (2)

Another way of releasing the past is to bury it symbolically.

1. Find or make an object which symbolises what you wish to leave behind: perhaps a photograph, a drawing, a letter, a coin or small item of clothing. (Avoid anything which would be toxic to the Earth if buried.)

2. Go to a place in nature which feels particularly sacred or powerful to you. (If it takes time and effort to get there, it emphasises the seriousness of what you are doing. I particularly love the wild energy of Dartmoor, and have buried many different objects there.) Take your object, a fork or trowel, and something as a 'give-away' to the Earth – perhaps some herbs, or a tiny crystal.

3. Having found your power spot, attune with Spirit, then dig a small hole in the Earth. Holding the symbolic object, call upon your unseen friends, and speak from the heart about what the object symbolises, what you learnt from this relationship, job, habit, emotional pattern, or period of your life, and why you wish to release it. If there is emotion to release, or words left unsaid, you can whisper or shout or cry or rage into the hole.

4. When you feel ready, bury the object in the hole, treading down on the Earth on top of it. Affirm that you are releasing this symbolic object to the Earth, and ask for Mother Earth to accept and transform it.

5. Sprinkle your 'give-away' on the Earth, or press it into the soil, giving thanks as you do so. Feel your new freedom as you walk away!

Step 7: Become your Future Self

Relax deeply, then imagine that you *are* your Future Self, that your Dream has come true. Notice how you feel. Then bring those *feelings* into your life as it is now – in whatever ways you can. For example, if your Future Self has a soulmate, and feels much more relaxed and confident than you do now, think about ways of making yourself feel more relaxed and confident *now* – perhaps meditating regularly, or having leisurely breakfasts, or taking a class in self-assertion, or going for a walk alone each day. You will then be magnetic to a soulmate, because you're taking on the energy, the vibrational frequency, of your Future Self. How would this Future Self take a shower, dress, go shopping, eat, socialise, think about work? As often as you can, try to *think*, *feel* and *act* as this Future Self.

The Basic Self is impressed by real live action in the world – so even if you have doubts, act 'as if' you expect your Dream to become reality! For example, if you're selling your house, start packing and put a removal date in your diary. If your Dream is to travel round the world, open a special savings account, buy some guidebooks and start planning your route. If you want a live-in partner, make space in your wardrobe, clear a shelf in the bathroom, have a spare key made – perhaps even set an extra place at your breakfast table! Throw out or give away whatever does not fit with the 'new you'. Take whatever action is necessary to convince your Basic Self that this *is* going to happen, that it is already in motion.

(Sometimes this happens in reverse. The Basic Self might send impulses to do something because *it* knows that a change is coming up. A week before I resigned from the Health Service, I found myself clearing out my office, and throwing out dozens of files that I would no longer need outside the Health Service. I had not even considered resigning at that point, and had no idea what was going on – but it felt good!)

Hopefully, it goes without saying that you also need to take any practical steps such as preparing for the job interview, revising for your exams, putting your house on the market, or meeting people if you want to make new friends! We *can* create miracles – but it makes life easier if we combine programming with a practical approach!

Step 8: Open to receive

It might sound obvious, but there is little point in trying to manifest something unless we are open to receiving it. Elspeth attended one of my 'Attracting a Soulmate' workshops, and afterwards went to a coffee shop in Hampstead. As she sat musing over her desire for a soulmate, an attractive man came in – and took the table next to her. After a few minutes, he smiled at her, pointed at the folded newspaper by her coffee cup, and asked, 'Is there anything happening in the world?' Elspeth found herself saying, 'I don't know – have my paper!', then she gathered her coat and *fled* from the café! Later on, she reflected that it had been a useful experience, since she had believed that she was open to meeting someone new until that moment of sheer panic!

As Lazaris often notes, 'Life is a gift, and ours is to learn how to receive gifts.' Yet how many of us turn our backs on opportunities, feel awkward about receiving gifts or compliments, undervalue what we already have or even deny that life itself is a miraculous gift?

Feeling unworthy or undeserving, our natural tendency is to try to *earn* something, to *work* for it, rather than being willing to receive it. Yet this is now becoming a crucial lesson for us to learn. Our world urgently needs the magic of receiving.

Opening to receive is 'high magic' as opposed to low or sympathetic magic. (The latter is outlined in steps 1-7 above.) It is the magic of the awakening Goddess. However, it isn't a short-cut to creating what we want. It is the *next step on* from 'low magic' – which allows us to create even more wondrous possibilities, or finally to clear blockages which we have worked on, *after* we have completed the earlier steps.

OPENING TO RECEIVE

(This is a powerful technique I learnt from Lazaris.') First, decide what you are willing to receive – perhaps work that you enjoy, or more love, or help in resolving a relationship difficulty, or releasing your self-pity, or closer contact with your Higher Self, or whether you wish to 'open to receive' in general.

Relax deeply, then meet or connect with your guide (or your Higher Self). (See Chapter 7.) Ask your guide how to *begin* and how to *end* this process. Your guide might suggest, for example, that you prepare by having a shower then lighting a candle, and that you finish by planting six black peppercorns in the garden, or going for a moonlit walk.

When you are ready, prepare in the way that your guide suggested. Then relax deeply, and imagine that you are in a peaceful place in nature. Use all your senses to find yourself there. Now find a way to descend into the Underworld, going deep down into the earth, perhaps by entering a tunnel, cave, treetrunk or well. Notice the sliver of crimson light at this entry point into the Underworld.

As you emerge into the landscape of the Underworld, you are greeted by your Higher Self – who leads you to a magical place. Tell

your Higher Self what you wish to receive.
Then simply allow it to happen. You might or
might not be aware of what is going on, but you
don't have to *do* anything. It might take five
minutes or an hour or so.

Then come out of the meditation, *knowing*
that you have opened to receive – and do
whatever your guide suggested to end the
process.

Step 9: Let go – and trust in the process of life

When we work on manifesting something, there is
usually a point where the processing and programming feel complete, when the energy drops away,
when it feels unnecessary or repetitive to do any more.
(It might only take half an hour to reach this stage,
or it might take several weeks. You might need to
work through all eight of the above steps, or just
choose two or three.) At this point, let it go and put
it to the back of your mind – and get on with your
life.

This final step of 'letting go' appears to be crucial
– it releases the energy we have built up, and allows
that energy to manifest how and when it will. It is
a step of faith, of trust in the process of life. What
you want may not arrive in quite the *form* that you
expect, or exactly *when* you expect it – but if
you have completed the process, it *will* come,
unless your Higher Self has an excellent reason to
block it.

Since we cannot see 'the whole picture' of our
lives, there are times when we need to trust and

surrender. This does not mean being passive or apathetic. It simply means knowing that whatever happens is perfect for our growth. Metaphysics is not a way of predicting and controlling the future, nor of manipulating other people. It is a practical way of learning through experience about the magical nature of our reality.

That's it! That's the nine-step process for creating what you want. If you complete these steps, the essence of what you want *will* arrive.

Of course, we often go through these steps without being aware of it. It's a natural process. If you recall a time when you created something that you wanted – perhaps being offered a job – you might have used all of the above steps, without realising it. Working through the steps just means 'slowing down' the process of reality creation, so that we can see it more clearly.

It is not always necessary to work through all nine steps. If you wish to create a parking space, for example, one step is usually sufficient – such as visualising and expecting it, or simply asking for it and saying 'Thank you'. We often work much harder than we need to!

Another one-step approach to manifesting is to feel grateful for what we have. Giving thanks tends to magnetise more of the same – whether it is friends, work, leisure-time, good health or prosperity. (In Hawaiian, 'to bless' also means 'to give strength to'.) Gratitude is also a healthy alternative to feeling guilty. I remember Bob Geldof, founder of Band Aid, being asked whether he felt guilty when he saw the starving millions in Ethiopia and the Sudan. 'No,' he said. 'Just grateful.'

Once you do create your Dream – the job, the house, the soulmate, the money, the talking stick – *celebrate*! Congratulate yourself, give thanks to Spirit, and enjoy it! Then spend some time looking at *how* you created it. Did you work through all nine steps? Did you focus on one or more steps? Which step felt most powerful? Can you recall a time when the process didn't seem to work? If so, what did you do differently *this* time? Learn all you can from your success. Then pick on another White Rabbit to chase – and apply your knowledge to this new challenge.

It is important to have Dreams beyond the Dream you are focusing upon. For example, if you have set your heart upon getting your novel published, and have convinced yourself that you will then be happy and content for the rest of your life, your novel might never be published – because part of you fears that you will then stop growing, that life will become aimless and meaningless, or that you might even die. This is one reason why people often hang on to one 'problem' in their lives long after they have resolved every other issue.

If we don't have problems, we need to have Dreams – and as we approach those Dreams, we need to have new Dreams; and beyond our personal Dreams, we need to have *global* Dreams, which we dance towards in the same way. The secret of happiness lies in enjoying the process, smelling the roses along the way, and knowing that our journey *is* our destination.

There is a story about a monk who devoted himself to seeking God. He prayed and meditated for long hours every day, learnt sacred texts by heart, starved himself, became a hermit – he tried everything. One day, while he was walking in the woods, he came across a hut. An inner voice told him that God was in this hut. All he needed to do was walk in, and his search would be over. The monk stood outside the hut for a very long time. Then he turned – and he tiptoed away . . .

Everyone needs a White Rabbit to chase.

Everything is Our Friend

*Love is like the warm sun that shines on the ice; it
melts and dissolves any barriers, any areas of pain.
Like the ice, your fears turn to water and evaporate.*

(Orin[1])

One morning, as I sat down to meditate, I found
myself in a vast desert, accompanied by a brown bear.
The Bear pointed in the four directions, and I understood that we had serious work to do! My plans for
the day were put aside, as I was taken upon an epic
inner journey for the next six hours. Over and over,
I faced and befriended fearsome beasts and dragons,
armed soldiers, sticky spiders' webs, boulders which
threatened to flatten me, fire which wished to engulf
me, and many other challenges.

Towards the end of the journey, the Bear told me
that I was now ready to face my most terrible foe. I
braced myself, wondering what lay ahead – and
gingerly peered around the grey stone walls of the
castle. Then I saw my enemy ahead – and a chill ran
down my spine. Sitting on a wooden bench, quietly
reading a book, I saw *myself*!

Since we create our own reality, the only 'enemy'
we have is ourselves. As we all know, life is not always

sweetness and light – either personally or globally – but this is not because we are inherently wicked, nor because God has it in for us, nor because life is supposed to be difficult. It is because we are not in harmony with ourselves, because we refuse to love and accept parts of ourselves.

By learning to love ourselves, by wrapping every aspect of ourselves in a warm embrace, we can melt all the inner gremlins which destroy peace of mind, or block us from our Dreams: our fears and doubts, resentment, guilt, self-pity, self-importance, insecurity, clinging to the past, the need for approval, all of our secret payoffs and hidden agendas. And if we are in harmony with ourselves, we will be in harmony with others, and with our world.

Our gremlins are always trying to help, in their own limited way. Everything is our friend. Some of our inner selves are only three or four years old, and don't know how to handle adult life – but they *are* doing the best they can. If we stop battling with them, or hiding from them, or identifying with them, and instead accept and befriend them, our 'enemies' – inner and outer – can be magically transformed into our allies.

SEEKING LOVE AND APPROVAL

To a young child, the need for approval is as crucial as the need for food and shelter. After all, if our parents and other Big People don't approve of us, we might be ignored, abused, even abandoned. (And if a child *is* mistreated, it usually believes it must be its own fault, and that if only it learns to be 'good', the abuse will stop.) So we learn to conform, to squash parts of ourselves, to be 'good', so that the Big People will like us.

The trouble is, by the time we reach our 20s, 30s, 40s and 50s, many of us are *still* behaving as if other adults are Big People. We are still trying to be 'good', still using ways of seeking love and approval which we learnt in childhood – as if the world might stop spinning if we dared to be honest, if we dared to be true to our own hearts.

First and foremost, most of us learn to suppress, deny and distort our emotions. Our emotions are the Basic Self's way of creating inner balance and harmony in response to everyday life. Sadness is a natural response to hurt, loss and grief. Anger is a healthy response to injustice, or lack of respect. Fear is a natural response to threat and danger. Emotions only become 'gremlins' when they are *suppressed*.

Sadly, some people have used New Age philosophy as an excuse to squash so-called 'negative' emotions – to deny their sadness, hurt, rage, fear, loneliness, vulnerability, disappointment and longings – under the guise of being positive, or 'looking on the bright side'. But once we have chosen to be human, dealing with the whole range, depth and intensity of emotions comes as part of the package deal. We have to learn to welcome and honour *all* our emotions, in order to become whole.

E-motion is energy-in-motion, and is intended to flow through us, *moving* us to do whatever we need to do: to cry, to shout, to run, to laugh, to jump for joy. Our emotions help us to stay in balance. If you watch a small child cry, her eyes will rapidly fill with tears, she cries – then, sometimes within moments, she smiles and runs off again. Emotion moves through her, she expresses it, and it is gone. That is how it is supposed to be. That is healthy e-motion at work.

Unfortunately, most of us learn at an early age that our emotions have to be hidden away. It isn't 'nice' to be angry. It is childish to cry. It is cowardly to feel afraid. It is a nuisance if we are joyful and exuberant. 'Be good!' is the constant cry. So we slowly learn to be 'good', rather than to be ourselves – because we want to be loved.

By the time we are adults, most of us are expert at suppressing our emotions – by tensing ourselves, by keeping our breathing shallow, and through drugs, overwork and other addictions. Instead of flowing through the body to restore balance, emotions then become blocked energy, which creates its own set of problems. When emotions are squashed, distorted, disguised or hidden away, the energy is converted into inner gremlins – from depression to self-pity, from paralysing fear to self-righteousness, from physical illness to addictions.

SUPPRESSED ANGER

Let's take anger, for example. Anger is meant to be an agent of self-respect and self-assertion, a constructive force for personal and global change. It is a wonderful, powerful energy if it is allowed to flow, and motivate us to act. But if we resist anger – telling ourselves it isn't nice, or isn't 'spiritual', or that we have no right to be angry – then the emotion can be silently smouldering hours, weeks or even years later.

Suppressed anger – like any emotion – has to

emerge sooner or later. Unless we *feel* our anger, it turns into a gremlin. The most common telltale signs of suppressed anger are depression and/or anxiety, self-pity, blame and resentment, guilt, apathy and inertia, sarcasm and irritability, struggle and martyrdom, addiction to drugs, alcohol, work, sex, food etc., accidents (often an expression of anger turned against the self), cancer, arthritis and other diseases (see Chapter 6), having affairs, or violence and aggression. (Violence is *not* an expression of pure, clean anger, but a symptom of bottled-up rage and fear which has eventually exploded.) Since the world is a mirror, noticing any of these signs in people around us can also indicate suppressed anger!

One technique for releasing anger is to write a very angry, no-holds-barred 'letter' to the person(s) concerned – then burn it or flush it down the toilet. (Do resist the temptation to post it!) Or bash a cushion or punchbag, breathe deeply, and just 'pretend' to be angry until the e-motion starts to move, and takes on a life of its own. Or go jogging, and shout – inwardly, if there are people around – in time to each step: 'I hate you!', or 'How dare you!' or whatever your inner Child wants to scream.

Don't attempt to forgive someone for hurting you, or to understand why you created a traumatic event, until you have *first* dealt with your anger, hurt and other emotions. Always take care of your Basic Self before 'up-levelling' to your Higher Self – otherwise you will attract further events which will bring those emotions to the surface.

Anger does not have to be rational, it does not have to be reasonable. Emotions simply *are*. By feeling your anger, you are honouring your inner Child, your Basic Self. You are reclaiming part of your wholeness. If you just *think* 'It's OK to feel angry', your Basic Self is unlikely to take you seriously, but by taking physical *action* – writing letters, bashing pillows – you give a clear message to your Basic Self that it's now OK to feel angry, that the rules have changed.

You could also meet your inner Child in meditation, and allow it to express its anger in whatever way it wishes. (My inner Child likes smashing china, so I sometimes give her several long tables covered in white tablecloths, which are piled high with the *very best* china to smash! Sometimes she chooses to burst balloons.) If your inner Child wants to beat up the person who hurt it, even that is acceptable in the inner world – *as long as your intention is to release your anger, and not to hurt the other person.* It is always our *intention* that counts. If you're afraid that you might explode if you start hitting a cushion, an inner journey can feel a safe way to release your anger.

It might be appropriate to express your anger to the person concerned. If so, make sure you do it cleanly. 'Clean' anger is simply an expression of how we feel. ('I felt very angry and hurt when you criticised me in front of my friends.') 'Dirty' anger tends to be deliberately hurtful or manipulative, contaminated with the need to blame or punish. It usually focuses on the other person, rather than on our own feelings. ('You're always so critical and negative. What's your problem?' 'Why are you so determined to destroy my self-confidence?') It just makes the other person defensive, and is unlikely to resolve the issue.

If your *intention* is to be hurtful, it might be wise

to wait until you have cooled down before expressing yourself. Is your anger really directed at that person, or are you nursing resentment from the past? Or are they mirroring a disowned aspect of yourself? Honouring our emotions means acknowledging them, taking responsibility for them, *then* deciding what action to take. It does not mean splattering them over whoever happens to be in the firing line! After all, no one else can *make* us feel an emotion.

FEAR AS A GREMLIN

If a wild rhinoceros or a ten-ton truck is hurtling towards us, the appropriate emotion is fear. Fear is our natural response to danger, and stimulates adrenaline so that we can move quickly to escape the threat. So far, so good. Fear is simply a high-energy state – a state of excitement, which prepares us for action, or prevents us from taking a dangerous risk.

Whenever we face the possibility of growth and change, we feel fear – because we're facing the unknown. Research shows that people perform best when they are moderately anxious – fear/excitement brings out the best in us. Fear is not the problem. It is all a question of what we do with our fear.

Nancy has been asked to lecture at a large conference on her favourite subject. As she waits to speak, her heart is thumping, her mouth is a little dry and she feels butterflies in her stomach. Is she nervous? 'No,' she smiles, 'I'm excited.' Barbara is giving a lecture at the same event. Her heart is thumping, her mouth is a little dry and she feels butterflies in her stomach. Is she nervous? 'Yes, I'm petrified!' she wails. 'I don't know whether I can go through with it. I will never, ever do this again!' Physiologically, their response is the same – but Nancy *interprets* her emotion as excitement, and uses it to motivate herself, while Barbara interprets the *same* feeling as terror, blocks the energy and allows herself to be paralysed.

When we choose to grow through joy, we have to learn to enjoy fear! Growing through joy, reaching for our Dreams, means constantly facing new challenges, new opportunities, new situations. It means diving in at the deep end, rather than paddling along the shoreline. And that means facing fear. The question is whether we choose to *label* it as fear, which can paralyse us, or as the 'buzz' of excitement, which can move us. If we take a deep breath and *flow with* the energy of fear/excitement, it is always empowering and enabling.

Fear comes from our illusion of separateness. It comes from forgetting that we create our own reality. When we walk in the remembering – knowing that we create it all, knowing that we are loved, knowing that the only true Reality is love – how can we ever be afraid?

In one inner journey, a mountain lioness appeared and said that fear was blocking my progress. She took me on a perilous journey along a precipice, down into the depths of a canyon and through shooting rapids – then asked if I was afraid. 'No,' I told her. 'I always feel safe in the inner world.' 'Ah,' she replied. 'Then why do you feel afraid in the outer world, which you likewise create?' She had a point!

One way of befriending fear is to choose to do something which scares us – such as firewalking, parachute jumping, speaking in public, stroking a spider, learning to drive, telling someone you love them or asking for a promotion. It's amazing how liberating this can feel!

Another approach is to imagine your worst-case scenario. What is the worst that could possibly happen? What are you really afraid of? Imagine it as vividly as you can – then (most important) *see yourself handling the situation* and moving beyond it. Whatever happens, we have created it – and we can cope with it. However, we often need to reassure our Basic Self of this. That way, we won't need to create the scenario in 'real life'.

Fear is a magnet, so whenever we worry about the future, we are attracting that future towards us. Every thought is a prayer! So it is important to acknowledge and release our worries and fears. If I hear a worry run through my mind, I sometimes blow that fear into my hands, as if I am holding a frightened bird. Then I attune to Spirit, inhale trust and optimism – and breathe this into my hands to heal and transform the fear. Or I simply put a red cross through the mental image – and gently smile, to reassure my Basic Self that its fears are ground-less. Shining the light of awareness upon our fears is often all that is needed to dispel the shadows.

SHAME AND GUILT

Another gremlin is feeling ashamed or guilty – which often blocks us from our Dreams. Unknown to you, your Basic Self might harbour guilt about stealing a lolly from a sweetshop thirty years ago, and so delib-erately block you from ever having money to spare, or from setting up your own business. Or it might carry shame about simply being alive, having heard once that your mother nearly died during childbirth; so it gives you asthma, because it is reluctant to breathe.

The Basic Self cannot reason in an adult way, so its feelings of shame and guilt can be persistent, irrational and often puritanical. Many adults feel 'guilty' about having a holiday, eating a cream cake, making love, saying no to a request, being playful, going for a walk, not meditating regularly, having a lunch break, sleeping late, and a thousand other harmless acts, simply because they are clinging to shame or guilt from childhood which has spread into adult life.

Guilt is often resentment in disguise. When we feel angry, but believe we have no 'right' to feel that way, the anger is often converted into guilt. (Frank Lake[2] uses the wonderful phrase 'hardening of the ought-eries' to describe a tendency to act according to 'shoulds' and 'oughts', instead of following our hearts.) In this case, dealing with the guilt means acknowledging and releasing the anger.

RELEASING GUILT AND SHAME

Relax deeply, then find yourself in a peaceful place in nature. Ask your Basic Self to join you – and to show you any memories which make it feel ashamed or guilty. Reassure it that *whatever* it shows you, you will send it only love and forgiveness. Then sit and wait patiently . . .

The answers might come as memories, images, thoughts, feelings, sensations or symbols. Whatever comes up, feel love for your Basic Self. If specific events come to mind, perhaps offer a loving new perspective to your Basic Self. For example, point out how hurt, frightened, jealous or young you were at the time. Or convert the guilt back into anger. Or remind your Basic Self that it is OK to make mistakes, and tell it what lessons you learnt from that situation. Or reassure it that there is nothing to feel guilty about, since it didn't cause any harm. Or just remind it that it is loved, simply for being. (Occasionally the Basic Self wishes us to make amends in some way if we have hurt someone else, but it is often content just to be forgiven.)

Keep asking whether there is anything else to be released, until every memory has been cleared, right up to the present day. (This might take two or more sessions.)

Now walk with your Basic Self in search of a fountain – a magical fountain made of crystal, with water cascading down. This is the Fountain of Grace. As you step into this sparkling fountain with your Basic Self, immersing yourself in its waters, you will be released from the past, forgiving yourself and others. You will know that you are meant to be here on the planet, and that you are loved. Bathe in the Fountain of Grace until you can really *feel* this emotional shift. Then gently come back to the room.

DOUBT AND CONFUSION

Doubt has a positive and a negative side. On the negative side, doubt can be disguised fear. It can become an excuse for not changing our lives, or our beliefs. ('I won't change until I've no doubt at all that I'm doing the right thing.' 'I won't believe it until you can prove it to me.') Doubt can be a way of clinging to the past.

The positive side of doubt is that it makes us think. If someone informs you that they're channelling a blue whale from Antares, or that they only betrayed you because you abused them in another lifetime, or that God abhors contraception or homosexuality, it's as well to be sceptical! Doubt can prevent us being gullible. On the other hand, if someone who seems intelligent and sensitive tells you that fairies and elves exist, it might be appropriate to doubt your 'commonsense' and keep an open mind.

Doubt can help us to pause, to consult our inner wisdom, and to integrate our intellect and intuition. It helps us to pose new questions, to review our old beliefs and attitudes, and to challenge dogma. (I remember Germaine Greer saying that she always tries to confuse her students, since once they are confused, they start to think.) Our beliefs always need to be flexible and open to change. Nothing is written on tablets of stone. Even the belief that we create our own reality will eventually be superseded by an even higher truth.

Throughout my years as a clinical psychologist, I remember briefly reaching points of clarity about my work – then along would come new clients and new ideas, and I would be thrown back into confusion.

Gradually, as I completed more and more of these spirals, I came to welcome these periods of creative paradox and confusion – which still continue today.

One of my spiritual teachers, DaBen,[3] suggests that confusion is a very high spiritual state. After all, confusion is a sign that old structures are being challenged, that former certainty has given way to doubt. Out of the shake-up, something new is bound to emerge.

SELF-IMPORTANCE

Another inner gremlin is self-importance – which is just a distorted way of asking for love. The Ego likes to puff itself up, to see itself as different or 'special', in order to handle feelings of unworthiness, and keep others at a safe distance. It is like a young child strutting around in its parent's shoes, trying to feel like a Big Person, but secretly feeling a fraud. (Feeling 'special' is quite different from having a healthy sense of pride in oneself.)

In spiritual circles, self-importance can take the form of being rather precious or earnest about spiritual growth, or seeing our services as indispensable, or even believing that we are destined to save the planet! On inner journeys, people sometimes meet cartoon characters, and I've noticed that this is often a message to 'lighten up', and stop taking themselves so seriously.

A common symptom of self-importance is being 'too busy' to relax and have fun. (Is there *really* something more important to do than playing with a child, or cuddling your dog, or enjoying the sunset?) Busyness often goes hand-in-hand with perfectionism: expecting yourself or your life or your work to be 'perfect'. Perfectionism is not a virtue. It is a way of seeking approval, and trying to feel 'better than' others, in order to cope with shame and unworthiness. It is also a path of growth through struggle. Since perfectionists are never satisfied, they are never at peace with themselves, never able to love themselves, and never able to accept others as they are.

The other side of the coin is false humility – what I term the 'miserable earthworm' syndrome. ('Oh no, I couldn't possibly . . .' 'Why would he want to spend time with *me*?' 'Oh, I'm not nearly as talented as the others.') Many of us worry about becoming arrogant or egotistical, yet false humility is another form of vanity and egotism – and prevents many people from fulfilling their life purpose. It is often a good excuse for staying safe, avoiding new challenges or getting stuck in blame or self-pity.

Another symptom of self-importance is making simple things either complicated or difficult. Our Ego loves the notion of countless years of psychoanalysis, complex magical or religious rituals, incomprehensible jargon and psychobabble – not to mention lots of arduous struggle! The Ego is always valiantly trying to impress (in a cack-handed attempt to protect and heal our inner Child), so it strives to feel one-up on other people.

An excellent remedy for self-importance – whether we feel 'better than' or 'less than' others – is learning to laugh at ourselves, and injecting a sense of fun into everything that we do. Whenever I catch myself being over-serious, pompous, perfectionist, workaholic or playing the 'miserable earthworm', I just start giggling at myself. It works every time!

VICTIMS AND MARTYRS

When we are very young, it often feels risky to express feelings such as hurt and rage. After all, the Big People probably won't approve – and what might happen then? A common way of coping is to convert these feelings into self-pity and self-righteousness. ('It isn't fair!' 'I try so hard, and no one appreciates me!') By the time we are adults, this pattern has often become a habitual way of being-in-the world. We have learnt to play the dangerous games of victim or martyr.

Victims give away their power by blaming others, or the past, or the government, or circumstances, or fate, or bad luck for what happens in their lives. Sadly, many victims create one disaster after another, because it is the only way they know of asking for love and support, and releasing their hurt and rage. Whenever we feel sorry for ourselves – as adults in Western society – or that something just 'happened' to us, beyond our control, we are playing the victim.

Martyrhood is a more sophisticated version of victimhood – the adolescent version of a childhood game – but it is just as destructive. Whereas victims tend to whine, martyrs just sigh a lot! Whenever we feel – *even slightly* – weighed down by responsibilities, hard-done-by, misjudged, mistreated, hopeless, misunderstood or unappreciated, we are playing the martyr. ('I have *so* much to do, but I'll get through it somehow', 'No, I'm fine – don't worry about me!') The self-righteous martyr within us feels it is saintly to struggle, often denies that anything is wrong, is very defensive – and tends to make everyone else uncomfortable. Martyrs rarely accept help and support, since they don't want to feel grateful to anyone ('Thanks, but I've already tried that', 'No, I can manage!'). Whereas victims tend to focus on the past, martyrs live for a golden future which is always just beyond reach.

Tom has been made redundant three times, and recently lost his home ('I guess I'm just unlucky'), but he is always willing to lend a helping hand. He attracts 'lame ducks' who need support, willingly lends money he cannot afford – and rarely gets it back. Tom is stuck in the victim-rescuer-persecutor triangle. He helps others in an attempt to raise his low self-esteem, while also 'staying safe' by keeping his distance – and instead just becomes a martyr/rescuer. (Unless we love ourselves and feel empowered, how can we love and empower others?)

There is a thin line between helping someone and disempowering them, or reinforcing their victimhood, and whenever we feel 'better than' or 'less than' the other person, we cannot truly help them. The more we try to 'rescue' someone, the more we paradoxically *block* change; and all too easily, we switch roles and become their persecutor, as resentment builds up on both sides.

The victim-martyr is a particularly common pattern among helping professionals and housewives, whose lives revolve around others' needs, but almost everyone has a streak of it. And underneath it all is a hurt and angry child – afraid of intimacy, yet longing for love.

CLINGING TO THE PAST

The only risk in getting in touch with blocked-up emotions is that it can become addictive. After suppressing anger or sadness for years, learning to bash pillows, scream or cry feels really good. It makes us feel alive – almost like the 'high' of a drug. We might then search for more and more traumas from the past (or explore the same traumas time after time), because we are hooked. We can become professional neurotics, 'working through the past' as a lifelong vocation, and building our friendships upon shared problems and misery.

Unfortunately, wallowing in the darkness does not necessarily lead us closer to the light – and can be a disguised form of self-pity. We get what we concentrate upon, so if we focus upon problems (and the past) rather than solutions (and the future), we only attract more problems. Since we constantly recreate our past, we can even create fresh, *new* traumatic memories to 'work through'!

In Alcoholics Anonymous, they speak of sitting on our 'pity pot' – full of self-righteous resentment. I've certainly known people who have wept or raged for years without really changing, because they are not releasing genuine hurt, sadness and anger – and learning from it – but are stuck in self-pity.

The whole point of releasing our emotions, and unearthing our gremlins, is so that we can say goodbye to the past, and be fully present in the here-and-now. The Native Americans speak of 'erasing personal history' in order to set ourselves free – that is, dropping anything which binds us to the past. If we nobilise the past – blaming our childhood, blaming our parents, blaming our partner, or blaming what happened yesterday or ten years ago for our present feelings or situation – then we condemn ourselves to repeat the old patterns again and again.

It is worth remembering that all of our gremlins are just mangled expressions of our basic childhood needs: the need for safety and security, and the need for love. Every problem is an attempted solution. We squash our anger and sadness because we long to be loved. We become paralysed with fear, or cling to the past, because we want to feel safe. We become workaholic because we are trying to 'earn' love and respect, and do not feel we deserve love simply for being. We get puffed up with self-importance because it is a way of keeping our fears, longings and self-hatred at bay. As we become aware of our gremlins, we should be gentle with ourselves – remembering that it is self-love which heals and transforms, not self-criticism.

Whatever our gremlins, the first step is becoming aware of them, and owning them as ours. This can take a great deal of courage and honesty, since it's much easier to kid ourselves that we're doing just fine, or that we 'don't feel any more anxious or depressed than the average person', or that we 'could stop drinking/overeating/undereating anytime', or that we work all day and night because we 'enjoy it'. We cannot love and heal our gremlins if we pretend they don't exist! First say hello to your gremlins.

The second step is to convert each gremlin back into its healthy original form (with the help of a good counsellor or therapist, if necessary). For example:

- If you are depressed, what are you angry about? Or what loss or change are you grieving about? Or how are you blocking your growth and change?
- If you feel anxious, which emotions are you backing away from? How can you use these emotions in a positive way, to make changes in your life? If you turned your anxiety into excitement, what would it 'move' you to do? What changes or decisions are you scared to make? How can you love and cherish your fearful inner Child?
- If you are workaholic, who are you trying to impress? Whose love do you want? What are you avoiding by devoting so much time to work? What do you fear might happen if you relaxed and let go?
- If you feel sorry for yourself, convert it back into anger, and let the energy flow. Use the e-motion to take charge of your life, instead of hoping that someone will rescue you, or fretting about the past, or daydreaming about the future.
- If you are bulimic, don't kid yourself that your problem is with food and weight. Look at the *real* issues: the gulf between your public self and your private self; your belief that your Basic Self is un-lovable; your inability to express anger directly, or to assert your own needs; your fear of intimacy, and yearning to be loved.

Whenever you feel uneasy, irritable, upset, depressed or numb, or notice any gremlin lurking around, the simplest approach is to 'sit with it'. Stop distracting yourself with busyness, food, TV or people – or criticising yourself for having gremlins – and instead, sit quietly.

Then imagine expanding around yourself, while also focusing on your heart and solar plexus area. (As a teenager, I remember using the terms 'Big Self' and 'Little Self' to describe this experience of expanding awareness towards one's Higher Self, while remaining aware of one's Basic Self. Sometimes I imagined that my Big Self was sitting on the moon, looking down at my Little Self – which usually helped to put life in perspective.) The crucial point here is to stop *identifying* with an emotion or thought ('I am in despair', 'I am frightened') and instead expand our consciousness *around* it ('Part of me feels despairing', 'My Inner Child is afraid'). That way, one no longer feels overwhelmed or out of control.

Once you have expanded into your 'Big Self', you might ask your Basic Self to reveal what the real problem is – then wait patiently. Anger, sadness, fear, hurt, jealousy, loneliness or other feelings might eventually bubble to the surface – or perhaps memories, or bodily sensations, or suppressed needs and desires. Whatever comes up, *welcome* it. If we love and honour any emotion, allowing its energy to flow deeply through us, it almost immediately starts to change. It is *suppressing* emotions which causes the pain.

> *The darkness needs to be seen,*
> *not as a threat,*
> *but as an opportunity*
> *to love.*
>
> (*Emmanuel[4]*)

OWNING OUR SHADOW

Whenever we feel that some part of ourselves is unacceptable, it is hidden away deep inside – only to re-emerge in a distorted form in later years. Whatever form it takes, our Shadow side will eventually come back to haunt us. In the meantime, it might turn into gremlins such as depression or self-doubt, reemerge as illness, 'accidents' or traumas, or appear as a 'mirror' in the outside world – all as a way of grabbing our attention.

For example, if you are surrounded by angry people – at work, in your family, or socially – perhaps you are suppressing anger? If your boss is always criticising you, perhaps you have unfinished business with a parent figure who was unsupportive, and your boss is helpfully drawing your attention to this? If you are fed up with friends or colleagues playing the victim – always moaning, feeling sorry for themselves, and blaming others – perhaps you too have slipped into the victim game? Or perhaps you are being the victim's best friend, a martyr?

The outer world is a mirror of the inner world – so whatever we see 'out there' is reflecting back our inner self. Our enemies are always our teachers, magnetised towards us because they can help us to reclaim our wholeness, to recognise and heal our gremlins.

I used to have a Friends of the Earth sticker in my car, and one day a scribbled note was left on my windscreen which read: 'Who are you kidding? You can't be 'green' and drive a car!' I was immediately filled with rage and guilt, muttered away to myself about all the work I'd done for Friends of the Earth, and wondered what sort of greener-than-green self-righteous person could do such a thing. My martyr was hooked! I quickly realised, with some discomfort, that the other person must be a mirror – and that if I was honest, I *was* being a teensy bit holier-than-thou in my life at the time, which is why my car had attracted that note!

Whatever annoys, irritates or upsets us in other people is sure to be an aspect of our own Shadow – and a crucial step in befriending our Shadow side is to recognise the frightened, dependent, vulnerable inner Child hidden beneath it. Almost all 'difficult' behaviour – from arrogance to selfishness, from bullying to self-pity, from perfectionism to being a doormat – is just a distorted way of asking for love and approval, protecting our inner Child, helping it feel 'good enough' or expressing its feelings. Once we can see through the disguise, and acknowledge what is going on, it is much easier to accept the behaviour – in ourselves, or in other people – and then the pattern usually changes.

The game of life is sometimes seen as a battle between the forces of good and evil, but the only real 'battle' is between love and fear. There are no evil people – just people with a wounded inner Child, who live in fear and separateness, and who try to *force* others to share their pain so that we know how bad they feel. The only 'darkness' is fear and ignorance – and if we shine the Light of love, awareness and wisdom upon our darkness, all that remains is the Light. As we learn to love and accept every aspect of ourselves, we will no longer need to project 'enemies' on to the outside world.

Of course, other people can also mirror *positive* aspects of our Shadow. Natalie came to see me because she lacked self-confidence. Part of the problem was that she had two grown-up sons, one of whom was very wise and knowing, and the other highly intelligent and academic. By comparison, she felt naive and stupid. I reminded her that the world is a mirror, and that her sons were reflecting aspects of her own Shadow side – her own wisdom, her own intelligence – which she was denying.

If we remember that the world is a mirror, it is impossible to slip into *either* being critical and judgmental *or* idealising others, since we know that *everyone* is an aspect of our own wholeness. We are all One. We are gazing at our own reflection!

OWNING YOUR SHADOW

Relax deeply, then imagine that you are alone in a house. It is a dark, moonless night, and you have only a candle to light your way. Use all your senses to find yourself there, and begin to explore. Within this house, you will discover all of your Shadow selves – the parts of yourself you have hidden away over the years, and need to re-integrate.

First, gather your courage and climb down into the cellar (which symbolises your childhood and the distant past). In the flickering candlelight, search for your Shadow selves – which might appear in any form, from a ghost to a goblin, from a magician to a magpie, from a soldier to a crippled child, from a vampire to a fairy godmother. (You might or might not know what each represents.) Greet each Shadow self in a loving way, saying that you have come to take it into the Light. Keep searching until you are sure that you have thoroughly combed the cellar – then ask your Shadow selves to go upstairs to the ground floor, and follow them up.

Repeat the same process on the ground floor (which symbolises your current and adult life), greeting any Shadow selves which have been tucked away. Search carefully in broom cupboards, wardrobes, dark corners – everywhere.

Now ask *all* of your Shadow selves to go upstairs to the attic (symbolising your future, and your Higher Self). When you are quite sure that everyone has gone upstairs, follow them up. The attic has huge windows, and is flooded with light. Form a circle with your many selves, and welcome them back into your consciousness. Dance and celebrate your new-found wholeness! Then gently come back into the room.

(This inner journey is based upon a recurring dream I had, over many years, about a haunted house. When I eventually plucked up courage to re-enter the house in a waking dream, and encounter my Shadow selves, it was a powerful and moving experience. I have since used the journey in many workshops.)

PSYCHIC CONTRACTS

Another form of gremlin is the 'psychic contract' – an agreement we made long ago, at a subconscious level, in order to seek love and approval (usually from our parents). Psychic contracts are often established by the age of three, and might be quite irrational – but a sub-clause of every contract is that we *forget* that we signed our name in blood, and therefore stick to the contract without being aware of it.

Examples of a psychic contract might be: 'I promise that I'll never be happily married, since you and Daddy weren't happy.' 'I promise that I won't have a successful career *and* a happy marriage, since you sacrificed your career for me.' 'I promise that I'll never leave you.' 'I promise that my life will always be a struggle, like yours.' 'I promise I'll never get angry.' 'I promise that I'll succeed only at things that you approve of.' 'I promise that I'll never really grow up.' Needless to say, such contracts can have a devastating effect upon our adult lives.

At a soul level, a psychic contract is always our friend. It offers an opportunity to learn a crucial lesson – such as the difference between love and martyrdom, how approval-seeking can block our growth, or the need to take responsibility for ourselves. Many of our relationships – with parents, with friends, with lovers, with colleagues or with neighbours – are underpinned by a 'psychic contract' which can become the central issue of the relationship: for example, one person might agree to be the 'persecutor' and another the 'victim', or a couple might play out dramas over trust and betrayal, or codependency issues, or freedom and responsibility.

(Of course, psychic contracts are just one source of relationship difficulties. Another common source is limiting or negative *beliefs* such as: 'No one will ever really love me', 'If someone loves me, they will always know automatically what I need and how I feel', 'People never get angry in a good relationship', 'If there's a problem, it's always his/her fault', 'If I get too close to someone, they'll die or abandon me', 'Men are always like my father/Women are always like my mother' – and so on.)

Carole's pattern was that she always chose men who were unwilling to commit themselves. She had now fallen in love with a man she hoped to marry, but he seemed to be backing off – and Carole was determined to understand and resolve this pattern. In an inner journey, Carole asked for a symbol of their relationship, and found herself by a waterfall. A beautiful golden globe came spinning out of the fast-flowing water, and she caught it with a sense of delight. Then she realised that she was holding the globe so tightly that it could no longer spin, and its dazzling beauty had grown dim – so she released it again, and let it fly. The message was clear: let go, and trust.

There is a Zen saying: 'Grab hold lightly; let go tightly.' The more we cling to a relationship or an object, the more likely we are to lose it. We have to learn to receive with an open hand, leaving everyone and everything free to flow in *or out* of our lives – knowing that whatever happens is perfect. (In an intimate relationship, this gives an air of trust and self-confidence which is usually magnetic to the other person!)

Another common pattern is to give away our power by insisting that it is the *other person* who has to change. In the Seneca tradition, whenever one points a finger in blame, three fingers point back – it is *you* who needs to change! (Olivia used to despise her husband for being 'weak and dependent'; but when she left him, she was forced to confront her own dependency needs. She realised that she had been rejecting her inner Child for years, and projecting it on to her husband.)

Once one partner has learnt the lesson – perhaps honesty and openness, or self-respect, or giving up self-pity, or learning to be intimate, or taking responsibility, or learning to let go, or handling anger in a constructive way – then the contract dissolves. (It takes two to keep a contract going.) At this point, the relationship might end, or move to a new level of closeness and commitment.

In any personal relationship, our real task is to learn how to love: how to love and honour ourselves, and how to love and honour the Other. We often get stuck because we are afraid of hurting others if we change – perhaps by learning to express anger, or becoming more independent, or by ending the relationship. Usually, the truth is that we are scared.

The spiritual law is that whenever we choose to grow – whenever we follow our hearts – it is the highest choice for everyone involved. If you decide to leave a marriage which is no longer working, for example, then it isn't working for either of you (nor for your children) – even if your partner protests at a personality level, and begs you to stay. If you decide to change your job, despite your current boss or colleagues claiming that they 'need' you, you are giving *them* the opportunity to grow and change. In any situation, there is usually one person who is more willing to grow, more willing to take a risk. The crucial question is whether we are acting from fear or resentment – and perhaps obeying subconscious patterns and contracts – or whether we are listening to our hearts.

DISCOVERING YOUR PSYCHIC CONTRACTS

Relax deeply, then imagine that you are on a deserted beach. Use all your senses to make the scene come alive – seeing the ocean, hearing the crashing waves, feeling the texture of the sand, tasting the salty air. Now find a way of descending into the earth. You might find an opening in the beach, which leads down a winding staircase made of sandstone. Or you might enter a cave, and find a passageway which goes deep underground. Or perhaps you will dive into the waves, and swim down into the depths of the ocean. Use your imagination to find a way of descending to the Underworld.

Once you emerge into the underground landscape (or seascape), look for a suitable meeting place – somewhere you feel safe and comfortable. Now repeat to yourself, *three times over*, 'I am now ready to remember and release my psychic contracts.' Then mentally ask your inner mother and father to join you. (They might come together or separately, and might or might not look like your real parents.) Ask each in turn, 'Did I make a psychic contract with you which is still having an impact?' They will answer Yes or No. If the answer is yes, ask whether they will reveal the contract(s). If not, start guessing what the contract might be. By examining the patterns in your life, you can probably make a few shrewd guesses, or ask for help from your guide. Keep trying until your inner mother and father have confirmed the contracts you made.

The next step is to clarify the lessons that you need to learn, so that you do not have to learn these lessons in other ways. (Again, you might wish to call in your guide or Higher Self to help you.) How would you know that you had learnt these lessons? How would you feel, think or act differently as a result?

Now, if you wish to end the contract(s), talk to your inner mother and father about why you made the contract. Remind them that you were only three years old, that it was your way of seeking love and approval. Tell them about the negative impact that the contract is having on your life – and ask whether they will release you. They might argue that the contract is protecting you from disappointment, or failure, or the threat of intimacy. If so, reassure them that you can handle the consequences of ending the contract.

Once they have agreed, ask your inner parents to hand over the contracts(s), written on rolled-up parchment and signed by you. Take

each contract, read it and tear it up into tiny
fragments. Hold the pieces in yur hands, and
confirm that the contract is ended. Suddenly,
the wind begins to blow – and the contract is
blown away like dust, disappearing into the air.
Then take a beautiful sheet of parchment paper,
and a lovely quill or fountain pen, and carefully
write out a *new* contract, choosing your wording
carefully. Then roll up your new contract, tie it
with a smart ribbon, and hand it to your inner
mother or father for safe keeping. Thank your
inner mother and father for their help. Then
gently come back to the room. (This journey is
available on my CD: *Discovering Your Psychic
Contracts*.)

*Have faith in yourself, for you are a being of Light;
Have trust in the universe, for it is loving and abundant,
And everything that happens is perfect for your growth.
(Celeste[5])*

Every event is a self-created opportunity to learn
and grow. If we learn the lesson and act upon it, the
situation will change. If we haven't learnt the lesson,
or haven't learnt the *right* lesson, the situation will
repeat itself in differing scenarios until we do – not
because we're browbeating or punishing ourselves,
but because we want to learn and grow.

Growth tends to go in spirals. We face a challenge
at one level, seem to resolve it, then it comes up again
at a higher level, and so on. We might take a quantum
leap in growth – perhaps from a sudden insight, an

inner journey, a mystical experience, a powerful work-shop, an inspirational book – then within hours, days or weeks, we *seem* to be back where we started. It is time for the slower process of *integrating* the fresh insight, wisdom or experience into our everyday lives, at deeper and deeper levels.

Our chosen 'lessons' might be about changing our beliefs, or breaking psychic contracts, or facing our fears, or learning to express anger constructively, or developing trust and faith, or taking responsibility, or being true to ourselves, or healing our inner Child, or owning our Shadow, or opening to receive, or balancing our masculine and feminine energy, or whatever.

When we are finally ready to release an old pattern, it sometimes comes up in an even tougher form than before – as a helpful opportunity to confirm that we really *have* learnt the lesson! In the same way, if we make a decision to change, any unresolved fears and doubts are shaken to the surface. At this point, what Bartholomew[6] calls the 'discouragement committee' often appears – friends, family and others who advise more caution, get annoyed, frown or pout at our plans. We need to remember that everyone is our friend, and that they are simply mirroring our own fears and doubts. Our task is to silently thank them for being 'mirrors' – then follow our hearts.

LISTENING TO THE WHISPERS

The world is not filled with random, meaningless events. Every aspect of our physical reality is rich with meaning and significance – even the national and international news that we 'happen' to hear, or snatches of overheard conversation. What is more, if we learn to 'listen to the whispers', then our Higher Self does not have to shout at us. It won't need to send the same messages in louder, more obvious (and more distressing) forms such as illness, accidents and other traumas.[7]

Once we learn to see the outer world as a *symbol* – as a dream that we create – we truly step into the magic. A flood on our kitchen floor, for example, might be a 'whisper' about unresolved grief or sadness. A speeding fine might be a reminder to 'slow down' our pace of life. A parking ticket might be a warning about clinging to the past, or 'staying in one place for too long'. Dry rot in the cellar might be a message about unfinished business from childhood which is 'eating away' at us. Aquaplaning in a car might symbolise 'skidding over the surface' of our emotions. A fire might represent the conflicting *desire* for and *fear* of transformation – together with the belief that growth has to be traumatic. (Witness the fire at Windsor Castle, on the Queen's wedding anniversary, after a year of extraordinary 'growth through struggle' for the Royal Family!)

The Sufi wisdom speaks of the need 'to pound relentlessly at the door of God' – but as I see it, God/dess pounds relentlessly at *our* door, if only we have ears to listen and eyes to see. Every event, every situation, every challenge, every opportunity, every emotion, every desire, every fear, every person we meet, every word we hear, is perfectly designed to help us to learn and grow. Everything is our friend. Everything is meant to guide our way Home.

We do not have to learn the hard way. We were not meant to battle with ourselves or others. We can learn with love, joy, laughter and ease. A casual game of tennis, for example, might offer lessons about balance, trust, self-confidence, staying in the moment, harmony with our Basic Self, discipline, co-operation and positive thinking. Alternatively, we might choose to learn those *same* lessons by facing struggle and hardship in our lives.

This does not mean that we should beat ourselves up if we *do* create 'problems' – nor should we feel smug and superior when life is going well! One of the pitfalls of metaphysics is the belief that, since we create it all, life should always be perfect. If we were perfect, we wouldn't be here! The reality is that life is often messy, perplexing and full of surprises, that we often feel sad, angry or fearful, that we don't always create what we want – and moreover, that *all of this is 'perfectly' OK*!

6

Body Language

The body has a mind of its own!
(Deepak Chopra[1])

A friend and I had arranged to meet in a coffee shop
in North London. As we sat down at a table, Marie
winced with pain, and I asked what was wrong. She
told me that her left knee was badly swollen. 'Are you
angry with your mother?' I asked, slightly tongue-in-
cheek. She looked at me in astonishment, and asked
how I knew. Apparently her mother had phoned two
days earlier, inviting herself to stay for two weeks, and
Marie had felt unable to say no – a repetition of an old
pattern from childhood. Within hours, her knee had
begun to swell up ... The knee often holds so-called
'negative' emotions such as hurt and resentment,
particularly from childhood; the left side of the body
is the 'feminine' side, or the mother; and inflamma-
tion often signifies the 'heat' of anger. So I made an
informed guess that Marie was angry with her Mother.

The body is always our friend. If it becomes ill, or
has physical symptoms, it is trying to tell us something. Our job is to work out what the message is,

and take action. Then the symptoms tend to go away
– often immediately.

Unfortunately, the biomedical model – the Western
scientific view of illness – has brainwashed us into
seeing illness and disease as a random, meaningless
event. We are 'struck down' by 'flu, or 'victims' of
cancer or heart disease – as if we are the hapless
occupants of a faulty and unpredictable machine. If
you get a headache, take an aspirin – problem solved!
If you have a swollen appendix, whip it out – problem
solved! Symptoms are just a sign that your body is
'malfunctioning'. Within this model, there is no need
to ask the crucial question of *why* you became ill, or
what it might mean, or how your body might be
trying to help you. You simply remove the symptoms
– using drugs, surgery or radiation. End of story.

According to the biomedical model, illness is just an
unpleasant and unfortunate experience, best remedied
by chemicals and 'experts'. It is certainly not a self-
created opportunity for learning and growth. As a
result, much of our suffering is wasted, because we don't
'get the message'. Despite vast increases in expenditure
on health care, our health is not improving.

It isn't that the medical model is 'wrong', just that
its vision is very limited. Will we really find a cure for
AIDS, for example, by devoting billions of pounds to
microbiology research? Or does the answer lie more
in examining our negative attitudes towards sexuality,
facing our fear, guilt, shame and prejudice, learning
to love and care for each other as fellow human beings
whatever our 'differences' – and becoming more aware
of the impact of the mind on the immune system?

The body is not a machine, nor even a bundle of

biochemistry, but a conscious energy system. What is more, we create it! Strange as it may sound, we *create* the physical body, moment by moment, with the power of our consciousness. Consciousness creates everything. The body is 'just' a highly energised thought-form. Thus, no illness or symptom can ever be random or meaningless. It is a direct response to your inner self, a mirror of your state of mind. The body responds to every aspect of you. And if you learn to listen to your body's whispers, it will never need to shout at you.

In my years as a psychotherapist, I noticed links again and again between people's emotional states and physical symptoms – as if the body were 'speaking' in its own language, reflecting the person's beliefs, fears, unexpressed feelings and desires. Rheumatism and arthritis seemed to go with bitterness and resentment, a strong tendency to be self-critical, and an inflexible approach to life. Those with low back pain were often perfectionists and martyrs, always running around after others, yet feeling burdened and secretly angry. Short-sighted clients often lacked a sense of direction – they didn't 'look ahead' far enough, or see the greater picture. People with 'weeping' skin disorders were often suppressing sadness or grief. Those with heart problems had major blockages around giving and receiving love or had 'lost heart'. Many others have spotted similar patterns of personality and dis-ease.

When I met Jennifer, I recognised her as a typical 'cancer-prone personality'. She was forty-two, married with two children – and had recently had a lumpectomy for breast cancer. She was referred to me by her bemused but willing GP, since she wanted to understand *why* she had developed cancer, in the hope of preventing any recurrence.

She was the eldest of three children, and remembers her mother as 'forever busy' – cleaning, cooking, tidying. From an early age, Jennifer was expected to care for her younger sisters. She grew up desperately trying to please her mother, and failing. On one occasion, her mother stopped her entering a ballet competition at the last minute because 'there was babysitting to be done'. Her father was away at sea for long periods, and Jennifer felt utterly alone.

At the age of seventeen, she met and married Robert – and for the next fifteen years, happily devoted herself to her husband and children. It was just when she was planning to start a career that her mother had a severe stroke. For the next six years, Jennifer dedicated herself to her disabled, incontinent mother. Then, within the space of six months, her daughter left home for university, and her mother had a second stroke and died. Less than a year later, Jennifer noticed a lump in her breast . . .

Research has gradually built up a profile of the 'cancer-prone personality': a childhood of frustration, isolation or despair, a tendency to please others at the expense of their own needs, and an inability to express anger and sadness.[2] Then there is an event which triggers the disease – usually the loss of a crucial role or relationship. Within two years, cancer is often diagnosed. The 'message' from the body is to learn to recognise one's own needs, honour one's emotions, and find a new meaning or purpose in life. Some people choose to do this, and their lives are transformed. Some 'choose' to remain ill, or to die –

and, of course, death is not a 'failure', just a chosen transition in consciousness.

Studies of people with 'multiple personality' have shown that one personality might be diabetic, while another – occupying the same body – is not. This clearly supports the idea that it is not the physical body which carries disease, but the personality. The body simply mirrors the personality.

WHY DO WE BECOME ILL?

Our natural state is one of glowing health and vitality. Whenever our body is less than healthy, it means there is a blockage or imbalance in our total energy system. This means that we are not loving and cherishing ourselves enough – that we are blocking our emotions or needs, or clinging to negative or limiting beliefs, or afraid to ask for what we want.

Often, ill-health is a sign of suppressed emotions. After all, if we refuse to feel our anger, hurt, sadness or fear, where can those feelings go? They're stored up in our body, along with the thoughts or experiences which triggered the feelings. This prevents energy flowing freely in that part of the body, and eventually causes symptoms and dis-ease, so that (hopefully) our attention is drawn to the unresolved issues.

Illness and dis-ease can also be a response to negative beliefs and attitudes. Whatever you think or say, your body is listening – and, like a trusting and innocent child, it *believes* you. So if you think 'This job will be the death of me yet', 'He's a pain in the neck', 'I'm sure I'm getting one of my migraines', or 'I always catch any bug that's going around', you can be quite sure that your Basic Self is paying attention – with predictable results!

Becoming ill can also be a way of indirectly getting what we want. The advantages of being ill might be fairly obvious – perhaps a few days in bed, lots of love and sympathy, avoiding unwanted commitments and obligations, or having time to relax. Some payoffs are less obvious, such as punishing your family or partner, wallowing in self-pity or having a ready excuse for failure. Some of us have learnt to be ill whenever we want attention or sympathy, or whenever we have to face an evaluation, or whenever we need a break, or whenever we're angry. Whatever the 'fringe benefits' of an illness, it is crucial to recognise your own pattern, so that you can ask directly for what you want, or give yourself a holiday, or face up to your fears, or express your feelings, or learn to say No – or whatever it is that your illness is doing 'for you'.

When I worked as a freelance journalist in my early twenties, I used to become ill whenever I needed a holiday. Since I worried constantly about money, I often worked seven days a week, and being ill was the only way I knew of giving myself a break. Eventually, I learnt to recognise the first 'warning signs' that I needed a rest – usually a hint of a sore throat – and take time off.

Finally, becoming ill (or having an 'accident') can be a way for our Higher Self to ensure that our life takes off in a new direction. I have seen countless clients over the years who have avoided change and growth with grim determination – until their Higher Self decided that the only way to 'wake them up' would be a serious illness or accident. It doesn't

Table of Chakras

Chakra	Centre	Endocrine gland	Emotional issues
1st	Base of spine	Adrenals	Security and survival; money and possessions; sense of belonging
2nd	Sacral (just below navel)	Gonads	Pleasure and sexuality; anxiety or guilt around these issues
3rd	Solar plexus	Pancreas	Suppressed emotions – especially anger, resentment, hurt, jealousy, sadness and fear; but also joy, happiness, enthusiasm and love. Self-esteem
4th	Heart	Thymus	Giving and receiving love. Self-love
5th	Throat	Thyroid	Communication, self-expression. Also known as the 'professional centre' (since our work is how we express ourselves in the world)
6th	Brow	Pituitary	Intuition
7th	Crown	Pineal	Our spiritual doorway

always work, and it is a last-ditch option, but many people can honestly say that getting cancer, or almost dying in a road accident, was a true blessing in disguise, catapulting their lives in an exciting new direction, or teaching them invaluable lessons.

Some people have traumatic experiences *despite* actively learning and growing. This is usually because, deep down, they believe that growth comes mostly through suffering. It's worth stating that illness and accidents are never – *never* – a 'punishment from God', nor an unavoidable karmic debt. God is unconditional love and makes no judgments, knowing that we are always doing the best we can. God lovingly accepts any mistakes we make on our journey Home. *We* make the judgments. *We* cling to guilt. *We* choose our karma – sometimes punishing ourselves for mistakes made in other lifetimes (not realising that all lifetimes are simultaneous, and that we can *change* the past, or simply choose to learn the lesson!). And we do sometimes *punish ourselves* through illness and accidents, since we have not yet learnt to love ourselves unconditionally.

THE SEVEN CHAKRAS

Good health and vitality depend upon *energy flowing freely* throughout our body. This means allowing our emotions to flow, allowing our ideas to flow, allowing experiences to flow, allowing life to flow through us – welcoming growth and change, and living in the moment, rather than clinging to the past. It means learning to give and receive love, and trusting in the process of life.

The body has seven major chakras, or energy centres, which are based along the spine – from the tailbone up to the crown. Each chakra is associated with a layer of the auric field, that multi-layered energy system which surrounds and interpenetrates the physical body. The chakras are also linked with specific emotional issues, and with certain parts of the body. The kidneys, for instance, are organs of the 2nd chakra, linked with pleasure and sexuality. If you are afraid of your sexuality, or feel guilty about enjoying yourself, or mistrust happiness, believing that it cannot last, your vital energy will become blocked around your 2nd chakra, and your body might express your fears through a kidney problem.

OPENING YOUR CHAKRAS

Opening the chakras increases the energy flow in and around the body, and therefore improves our physical, mental and emotional health.

A simple but powerful way to energise and balance the chakras is one I learnt from Lazaris.[3] Imagine each chakra in turn spinning, and becoming larger, starting with the 1st chakra. (Let them spin in whatever direction feels right; they usually spin in alternate directions.) At the same time, picture an explosion of coloured light of the appropriate colour. (The colours go from red (1st) to violet (7th) like a rainbow.)

1st   Tighten your anal sphincter, hold briefly, then relax. (TOMATO RED)
2nd Curl your toes, then relax. (ORANGE)
3rd Hold your stomach in, then relax. (SUN-FLOWER YELLOW)
4th Tap your thymus gland, on your upper chest, a few times with one hand. Alternatively, just smile! (GRASS GREEN)

5th Swallow. (SKY BLUE)
6th Close your eyes, and look up. (DEEPEST
     BLUE-INDIGO)
7th Imagine VIOLET or WHITE or GOLD light
     (or a mixture of these) around your crown.

This exercise only takes a minute. I've used it
while going up or down in a lift, or waiting at
traffic lights. (There's no need to close down
your chakras afterwards, despite the common
scare stories about 'leaving yourself open'.) Use
the exercise regularly for best results – weekly,
at least.

   If you want to draw upon the energy of a
chakra, close your eyes and focus on that part of
your body. Move your consciousness 'inside' the
chakra. Then imagine you are bathing in the
colour of that chakra. (If the colour which feels
right is not the 'proper' colour, trust your
intuition.)

• 1st chakra – for grounding yourself, or
                feeling safe and secure;
• 2nd chakra – for pleasure and sexuality;
• 3rd chakra – letting your emotions flow,
                being energised;
• 4th chakra – feeling loving and
                compassionate;
• 5th chakra – for communication and
                self-expression;
• 6th chakra – for intuition;
• 7th chakra – for expanding consciousness,
                gaining spiritual perspective.

BODY LANGUAGE

What does it mean if you have a headache, or twist an ankle, or have dry, scurfy skin? Well, everyone is unique, with their own unique body language – and only *you* can know what your own symptoms or diseases mean. However, the patterns and themes shown below are common enough to be used as a starting point when you want to 'think' in body language. *Do bear in mind that this list is rather like a dream dictionary – useful as an initial guide to possibilities, but not to be taken too seriously!* The best guide to what *your* illness means is your own intuition.

From head to foot

Headache

Conflict or indecision – often wanting to do one thing, but feeling you 'should' do another

Migraine

Conflict, suppressed resentment, perfectionism

Eyes

What don't you want to see? Short-sighted – not looking ahead enough, not seeing things in perspective; long-sighted – living in the future, ignoring details; astigmatism – distorting your reality; glaucoma – feeling under pressure; suppressing all emotions

Ears/deafness

What don't you want to hear? Not hearing inner guidance

Neck pain

Who or what is 'a pain in the neck'? Inflexibility; indecision

Throat

Not expressing yourself verbally; resistance to change, or to starting your 'life's work'

Shoulder pain

What are the burdens you are carrying? Are you carrying others' worries or responsibilities, at your own expense? Are you willing to let go, or to seek help and support?

Breasts

Mothering, nurturance, femininity

Heart

Blockages around giving and receiving love, or feeling the joy of life; 'loss of heart'

Lungs/asthma

Feeling smothered, overprotected; suppressed tears; feeling you have 'no right to breathe'; feeling unworthy; blockages around giving and receiving; ambivalence about being here

Pancreas

Where we store our feelings

Liver

Where we process and sort out our feelings. (Alcohol

– which attacks the liver – can be used as a way of avoiding looking at our feelings, but at a heavy cost)

Stomach/vomitting
Something you can't stomach; being asked to take in new idea(s) or experience(s) which you 'cannot digest'

Ulcers
Fear; being 'driven', perfectionistic; feeling unworthy

Hands
Linked with giving (right hand) and receiving (left hand); holding on, and letting go; reaching out to others

Elbows
Suppressed hurt or resentment; inflexibility

Back pain
Feeling hurt, unsupported; suppressed resentment, self-pity; trying to be perfect; taking yourself too seriously

Hips
Stubborn anger

Diarrhoea
Not allowing yourself to be nourished; refusing to 'take in'; running away from something

Constipation
Clinging to the past; holding back emotions; refusing to let go; lack of trust

Incontinence
Feeling out of control

Venereal disease
Guilt over sexuality

Cystitis
Feeling 'pissed off' (especially with your partner)

Tailbone injury
Worries about survival and security – e.g. financial worries, fear of mortality, or fear that you 'cannot survive' without your partner, your house or your job

Legs
Our mobility; our willingness to move forward

Knees
Stubbornness, inflexibility; hurt/resentment from childhood

Ankles
Linked with pleasure and sexuality (2nd chakra)

Feet
Staying grounded; security and survival (1st chakra); 'best foot forward' – stepping into the future

Left side
Connected with 'feminine' aspect of self, and mother

Right side
Connected with 'masculine' side of self, and father

General conditions

Accidents

There is no such thing as an accident! Usually comes from anger turned against the self; need for a break, or a change of direction; need for sympathy and support

Allergies

Seeing world as a threat; lack of trust; not owning your power

Alzheimer's disease

Shutting down; escaping from the world; running away from emotions

Arthritis/rheumatism

Resentment, bitterness; self-criticism; inflexible approach to life

Blood disorders

Linked with 'blood relatives' (i.e. whoever your define as your family); emotional problems or conflicts within these relationships

Blood pressure – high

Suppressed anger and resentment towards family members (e.g. partner, parents)

Blood pressure – low

Giving up; lack of commitment to being in the world

Broken bones

A broken bone suggests that your basic 'support structure' feels under threat – perhaps your family, your career, finances or self-image; or that you are trying to break free – but it feels dangerous. (Notice what the broken bone has stopped you doing, or what it has postponed, for clues about what you're afraid of doing)

Cancer

Suppressed grief and resentment; feeling hopeless/helpless; lack of meaning or purpose; suppressed need for 'growth'; fear; something 'eating away' at you. (Notice where the cancer is for further clues)

Common cold

Self-pity; suppressed tears; need for a break; confusion and uncertainty; release of toxins

Fever

Suppressed anger

Hypoglycaemia

Trying to be perfect; demanding too much of self/others

Immune system deficiency

Lack of self-confidence; feeling powerless or defensive; trapped in self-pity; yearning for love

Inflammation

Suppressed anger

Oedema (holding on to fluids)

Not letting go of the past; feeling the need for protection

Premenstrual syndrome

Uneasiness about womanhood; not trusting in the natural flow of life; not owning your power

Sinus problems

Suppressed tears/grief; irritation with someone

Skin problems

Connected with self-image, how you present yourself to the world; red/inflamed skin conditions, boils, burns – suppressed anger; 'weeping' skin conditions – suppressed grief; dry, scurfy skin – cutting off your emotions, living too much in your head; spotty skin – adolescent issues (e.g. personal identity, fear of losing control, conflicts over sexuality and intimacy, self-acceptance)

Stiffness

Being inflexible, stuck in your ideas

Stroke

Refusing to trust in the process of life, to go with the flow; ignoring spirituality

Stubbed toe

Watch your footing; stay grounded

WHAT DOES YOUR ILLNESS MEAN?

Whatever your symptoms or illness, there are six steps to take in order to decipher your body's message, and know what action to take. Sit down with a notebook and pen, so that your Basic Self knows you are taking it seriously.

Don't *blame* yourself for getting ill, or beat yourself up for it. Just take responsibility for your illness, trusting that there is a good reason for it – and welcome the opportunity to learn and grow. (On the other hand, beware of glorifying illness as a learning process, or you might get hooked on becoming ill!)

First, work out the 'body language'. What metaphors is your body using? Which chakra is the affected part linked with? What is your body expressing in a symbolic way? What issues in your current life might it be linked with? Brainstorm the possibilities, and see which 'clicks' with you.

Second, what are the advantages of having this illness? Be honest with yourself. Is it offering you a couple of days to relax, or love and support from your loved ones, or an excuse to avoid an unwanted obligation or difficult decision? Or is it an excuse for failure, or a way of punishing someone, or an opportunity to feel sorry for yourself? Is it a rather poor way of saying No? If so, how could you get these advantages in a more healthy and positive way?

Third, what are the unmet needs or suppressed emotions which you have been ignoring? Which emotion(s) is your inner Child trying to express? Sadness? Resentment? Fear? Grief? Love? What unmet needs is your Basic Self trying to draw attention to? The need for warmth and affection? The need for fresh air and exercise? The need for more salads and fresh fruit? The need for a creative outlet? The need to feel needed? The need for recognition? The need for more challenges? The need for more fun and relaxation? In what way(s) are you not loving and cherishing yourself?

Fourth, what are the negative beliefs or attitudes which encouraged this illness to develop? How have you programmed your body to become ill? For example, 'I always get colds in the winter', 'Everyone's going down with flu at the moment', 'I have a family history of heart disease', 'I always feel ill after Chinese meals', 'You can't expect perfect health as you get older.' Beliefs such as these are far more dangerous than bugs and viruses!

In the nineteenth century, a physician swallowed a whole flask of active cholera bacilli, in order to demonstrate – successfully – that a healthy body will not succumb to infection and disease. Bugs and viruses don't make us ill – *we* do! Physiological factors can and do have impact, but in themselves are not sufficient to cause disease.

In Britain, private health insurance is an excellent way of programming yourself to be ill. After all, you are telling your Basic Self, 'I don't trust myself to stay fit and healthy. I expect to be ill some time', and your body will willingly co-operate with this. Just so that you can convince yourself that you're not wasting money, you are likely to require expensive hospital-isation, surgery or long-term care at some point. That way, you will get good value for money! Health insurance is built upon fear, and alienation from our Basic Self. How much easier and cheaper to change our beliefs: to see our body as a friend, and decide to stay healthy! (Sadly, much 'health education' simply spreads fear and negative beliefs, and thereby contributes to illness and disease.)

Fifth, ask yourself what *action* you need to take. What is the lesson which you need to learn, and how can you prove that you have learnt it? Understanding the message from your body is a waste of time unless you *act* on it! This might sound obvious, but I know how often I have received a clear message (such as 'Spend more time in nature', 'Drink more water', or 'Find a new creative/artistic hobby') and have still taken a year or more, despite frequent reminders, to act upon it.

Finally, focus on health rather than disease, and see yourself in perfect health. We get what we concentrate upon. The more we think about illness and symptoms, the more likely we are to create them. Above all make the *decision* to get well.

(*Note*: Children and pets are very sensitive to the energies around them, and often become ill in response to tension and conflicts in the home – so if your dog vomits or becomes agoraphobic, it's worth asking whether it is mirroring *your* issues. However, if a child dies of leukemia, say, it does *not* mean that you should wring your hands with guilt, since your child created that reality too. As a soul, your child had a contract to die young – and you had a soul contract to experience losing a child. The same is true of a child who is born handicapped. There is no blame – you simply chose each other.)

MEETING YOUR ILLNESS

Relax deeply, then imagine that you are in a forest. It is a moonlit night, and trees are silhouetted against the silvery light. Open your inner eyes, and see the forest around you. Hear the owls hooting, and feel the whispering breeze. Now look for a path which leads deep into the forest, and begin to walk along this path – stepping over fallen tree-trunks, pushing low branches out of the way, hearing the crunch of your steps on the leaves underfoot.

In the heart of the forest, you come upon a grassy clearing, brightly lit by the moon. You settle down in the centre of the clearing, and wait. Mentally, you ask for your illness (past or present) to come to you. It might take the form of a person, a creature or an object – or you might simply sense a presence. Wait for your illness to join you in the clearing.

When it arrives, greet it as a friend. Say that you are glad to see it, since you wish to learn from it. Tell it that you know it has (or had) an important message for you, and that you are eager to understand this message. Ask your illness what it came to teach you. Then wait patiently for its answer – which might come as words that you hear, as thoughts, as images, symbols or memories. Make sure that you are clear about what action you need to take – and ask the illness if it will leave you, if you take this action. If not, what else do you need to do? (Know that all the answers are within you. You created the illness, you know what it means, and you know how to heal it. You simply need to access your own wisdom.) Remember to thank your illness for its message.

> Finally, ask your guide to join you, and
> request healing. Your guide might heal you
> directly, or might work with your illness. Ask for
> the healing to continue during the coming days,
> weeks, months if necessary – and thank your
> guide. Picture yourself as healthy. *Feel* your
> body pulsing with health and vitality. Then
> gently come back to the room.

HEALING YOURSELF AND OTHERS

Another way of working with illness is to ask your
subconscious, your Basic Self, for a symbol of the
illness – and then change this symbol to one which
feels more positive, healthy and harmonious. An
important point is that the images you use should be
benign and friendly. If you create an image of a battle-
ground in which your immune system valiantly
charges at an invading hoard of bacteria – the white
knights vs the bad guys – you're reinforcing the idea
that the body has to 'fight' illness, and making it a
struggle. Instead, you might picture the white knights
taking the small, weak, confused bacteria by the hand,
and gently showing them the exit door, in the
assumption that they have lost their way. Make it easy!

When I suffered from tinnitus (ringing in the ears),
I decided to work with the symptom in this way. On
an inner journey, I found myself in a desert facing a
long row of monks in saffron robes, who were solemnly
ringing bells in unison. They were making a tremen-
dous din! I approached the monks, bowed to each
one in turn, and offered each an ostrich feather in

return for the bell. I moved along the whole line, replacing their bells with feathers, and left them all shaking their ostrich feathers in unison – in blissful silence! The ringing in my ears was much improved.

You can also give messages to your Basic Self through affirmations and rituals. Doctors generally use both techniques. They give you an affirmation such as 'I'm sure you'll find that these pills do the trick', or 'The problem will heal itself within a few days', and they might perform a ritual such as handing you a prescription, examining you, or performing an operation. People who have a child-like trust and faith in doctors generally find that any old pill or potion works miracles for them, confirming their belief in the wonders of modern medicine!

In one study of electroshock treatment – a horrifying treatment for depression in which people's brains are mildly electrocuted – it was discovered that one shock machine hadn't been working for several months, yet the outcome had been the same as usual! It was the ritual which 'worked', not the electric shocks. (How much modern surgery 'works' for the same reason? Having an operation is certainly a powerful – and traumatic – message to your Basic Self.)

Children are particularly responsive to simple rituals such as 'kissing it better', since they haven't yet learnt that magic isn't supposed to work! A few years ago, I visited a friend who was having severe marital problems. His little girl had an earache, so I asked her what the pain in her ear looked like. She told me it was a wriggling black insect with red eyes. I cupped my hands over her ear, and said, 'Ask the insect to leave and find another home, because this is *your* home.' (I knew that her earache was caused by the pain of overhearing her parents' arguments. Her mother was involved with another man – represented by the invading insect.) I clasped my hands over the 'insect' as it emerged from her ear, took it to the back door, and allowed it to 'fly away'. Her earache vanished with it.

Of course, whenever we use healing techniques or holistic therapies, it is important to 'get the message' – otherwise the symptoms will recur, or you will have to receive the message in another form. If we use, say, acupuncture or homoeopathy to relieve symptoms without also asking ourselves what *caused* the problem, or how the body is trying to help us, then it's just the 'holistic' equivalent of taking an aspirin or tranquilliser.

In Hawaii, I learnt a simple yet effective method of Huna healing known as 'kahi' (oneness). It can be used with children and adults, or even as a self-healing technique. All you need to remember are the power points of the body, and three steps for use.

The power points are: crown, brow, chest, back of neck, navel, pubic mound, base of spine, shoulders, hips, palms and soles. These are easy to remember, since they correspond to the seven major chakras, plus the 'corners' of the trunk (hips, shoulders) and the extremities (palms, soles).

The three steps of 'kahi' are:

1. Energise yourself – that is, get your own energy flowing well. A quick method is to rub your hands together briskly. (This has the added advantage of warming your hands before you touch your client!)

2. Put one of your hands on the affected area (that is, wherever the discomfort is), and the other hand on a distant but comfortable-to-reach power point. (For example, if it's a child with a bruised knee, put one hand on the knee, and the other perhaps on the child's forehead or shoulder.)

3. Focus on your hands, and breathe normally. *Don't* try to send energy, or try to *do* anything. Continue for a minute or two. (If your client doesn't feel any change within twenty seconds, try another power point.)

Healing occurs simply because you are completing a circuit of energy, so that energy starts to flow through the affected area again. If energy flows normally, there will be no symptoms. Try it – it works!

HEALING AT A DISTANCE

The same technique can be used to heal others at a distance. Hold an object which symbolises the person in your left hand (perhaps their name on a slip of paper), and a symbol of the energy or quality you wish to send in your right hand – perhaps a quartz crystal for general healing, or write it down on a slip of paper. Then just focus on your hands, breathing normally, for a minute or two.

While studying meditation in Nepal, a friend of mine staggered up the mountain at dawn for his regular morning session. He felt tired and drained, and was questioning why he was putting himself through this strenuous ordeal. Suddenly, he shot bolt upright as though injected with energy. He gazed around in amazement and saw, a hundred yards away, a Tibetan lama – who then bowed deeply in his direction, with a broad grin on his face. (A few days earlier, my friend had watched the same lama partially dematerialise while ringing a bell.)

All energy, all consciousness is interconnected, so healing at a distance is not a problem – unless our rational mind believes it is! I recently had lunch with a friend in a village pub, where we were served by a tense and morose barmaid. Sitting in the beer garden, we decided to send healing energy to her, to use in whatever way she wished. I imagined a shaft of light entering my crown chakra from above (so that I was tapping into the universal Source), then sent out beams of love and light from my heart chakra and brow chakra. I sensed that she was absorbing rather than rejecting the light. When we returned our plates and glasses to the bar, we were delighted to find her laughing and smiling with the customers, as if she were a different person! Coincidence? There is no way of knowing – but it's amazing how often sending love and light seems to be effective.

SENDING LOVE AND LIGHT

Attune with Spirit, then imagine a bridge of light coming from your heart and surrounding the other person in a bubble of light. (There is no need to know where the person is.) Stay centred in your heart, and say any words that feel appropriate – such as 'Please accept this light, using it in any way you wish/ using it for self-healing/using it to release the past/using it to connect more deeply with your Higher Self.' Try to sense whether the light is 'bouncing off' or is being accepted, and notice how this corresponds to any apparent change in the person. (Obviously, this shouldn't be used to try to change someone for your own benefit. Always affirm that the person can use the light or not, as they wish.)

CHANGING OUR DNA

One of the most staggering possibilities for healing is that of changing our genetic structure. As the New Age approaches, the DNA of humanity is undergoing profound changes, right across the world. Bizarre as it may sound, more and more people believe that it is possible to re-programme our own DNA, or to ask for unseen help in doing so.

I recently saw a woman who had travelled a long way for a consultation. I had seen her two months earlier, and since then her life had improved so greatly that she was unsure why she had come again. As we talked, she mentioned a genetic condition which she had inherited from her mother. I suddenly knew why she had come. 'Your guide would like to change your DNA structure,' I heard myself saying. Sure enough, her guide wished to take this opportunity to heal her inherited disease, and informed her that within six months she would notice a huge improvement.

In the past three years, I have found myself working

more and more with DNA structure – sometimes quite unexpectedly. Whenever we change our beliefs, attitudes, desires or emotional patterns, it is far more powerful and lasting if we ask for that change to be absorbed into our DNA, since our DNA carries the blueprint for our future. Simply ask for it to happen, and the process begins. Our DNA is not a *fixed* blueprint, but dynamic and ever-changing.

Whatever we want to change about our health, our body, our lives, we simply have to ask – and wait for guidance. We have scarcely begun to glimpse the potential of our human consciousness.

CHANGING YOUR DNA

1. Relax deeply, and imagine that you are breathing in white light – filling your lungs and chest with light. Slowly, the light fills your body, legs, arms, shoulders, neck and head. As you continue to breathe in, the light spills out beyond your skin, surrounding you in a bubble of white light. Allow the bubble of light to become stable at a certain size – whether it is six feet wide or twenty feet wide.

Now remind yourself of the physical or emotional condition that you wish to heal. Imagine that somewhere in the distance, there is the energy of healthy DNA which can replace your own. See or sense this energy, then call it towards you. Imagine the energy approaching and coating the bubble of light which surrounds you. Continue to call the energy into your body, and see or sense it seeping through your bubble of light. Feel it entering the body, and ask it to enter the DNA of your cells. Allow yourself time to absorb the energy. Relax and enjoy!

Finally, mentally ask whether you need to do anything to aid the healing process. (For example, when I worked on my inherited astigmatism, I was guided to relax the little muscles behind my eyes as often as I remembered. It's worth remembering that many 'inherited' diseases are not passed on genetically, but through emotional and behaviour patterns learnt from our parents.)

2. Alternatively, you can ask your guide for help. Meet your guide on the inner planes, and ask for healing for your DNA. Your guide might surround you in light, hold your hands while energy is transmitted, or touch your body.

(Repeat either approach as often as it feels necessary, until you sense that the healing is complete.)

Finally, remember that we *co-create* our reality. We are individuals, but we are not separate. The fact that *you* don't have AIDS, say, does not mean that it isn't 'your' problem. It is *our* problem. We have co-created AIDS as a global issue, and it has implications for everyone who is aware of it. It is worth asking yourself what AIDS, or heart disease, or cancer means to you. Why have you created it in your world? What issues does it raise for you? What opportunities does it offer *you* to learn and grow?

7

Our Unseen Friends

Some of us who no longer need to be human exist in our realm of consciousness to guide and to teach. Meet us as friends. Allow us into your lives.

(*Emmanuel[1]*)

In the early hours of the morning, a young woman called Sophie arrived at the bus station in downtown Los Angeles. It was her first visit to LA, and Sophie was eager to explore the city before her job interview. She ventured out into the dark streets and, before long, she was lost. Moreover, she became aware of three men lurking in the shadows, following her. Sophie suddenly knew that her life was under threat, and silently prayed for help. Then she noticed another man – tall, dressed in denims and carrying a lunchbox – walking towards her. Instinctively she ran to him for help, and was struck by the beauty of his face. 'Come, I'll take you to safety,' he said. As they arrived back at the bus station, she thanked him from her heart, and said goodbye. 'Goodbye, Sophie,' he gently replied. She walked inside, then it hit her. Sophie! How had the stranger known her name? She had not introduced herself. She ran out immediately – but the street was empty.[2]

There are countless true stories like this. Angels are usually seen as mythical creatures which belong to Biblical times, and seem somehow inappropriate amidst bus stations and skyscrapers. Yet when someone is in danger, a guardian angel *can* come to the rescue – often as an urgent 'inner voice', but sometimes in human form – whether or not we ask for help.

We are not alone in our Earth walk. We are not abandoned once we plunge down the birth canal. On the contrary, we are watched over, loved, protected and guided throughout our life's journey – and we can call upon unseen help at any time. We are surrounded by loving helpers. If we *do* face accidents, injury or premature death, it is invariably because it is part of our chosen destiny.

If we do ask for help, however, we should not expect booming voices from the sky, or creatures with huge flapping wings! There is a fable about a woman whose home was threatened when a river burst its banks. All houses in the area were evacuated, but when a policeman arrived at her door, the woman said, 'No, I am not going. God will save me.' The waters began to rise, and she was forced to move to the upper floor of her house. Then a man came along in a rowing boat, offering to row her to safety. 'No,' said the woman. 'God will save me.' Before long, she was clinging to the roof of her house, water lapping at her ankles. A helicopter came over, and threw down a line for her – but she waved it away. 'God will save me,' she shouted. The woman was swept away by the flood, and drowned. When she arrived in heaven, she was very cross with God. 'Why didn't you save me?' she asked. God replied that He had sent her a policeman, a rowing boat *and* a helicopter. What more did she expect?

Angels will only *materialise* when it is the best possible option – and even then, they tend to disguise themselves as human beings. Unseen help usually comes in apparently ordinary ways – a sudden hunch or inspiration, an inner voice, a 'chance' meeting, a suggestion from a friend, an unexpected change of plan . . . Many of the 'ordinary' events of our everyday lives are orchestrated by angels, guides and other Beings of Light.

Fortunately, we don't have to create a life-threatening situation to contact our unseen friends. We can speak to them at any time. They are just a thought away – and are only too willing to help in our everyday lives. (After all, whenever our guides help us, *they* learn and grow. It is a mutual relationship.)

Some spiritual traditions imply that there is a vast, uninhabited gulf between human beings and God/dess. This never made any sense to me. If life is a constant process of evolution, if we are forever learning and growing and changing, surely this process continues in other dimensions of reality? Surely there are countless 'stepping stones' between life on Earth and the creative Source?

Having witnessed many international mediums over the past fifteen years, I have no doubt whatever that we can communicate with people who are 'dead' – but it is equally clear that death is just one more step along the road. We do not become totally wise and loving just because we are dead! Indeed, many of those on the astral plane are confused or stuck, or muddling along rather aimlessly, and can benefit from *our* wisdom and guidance. But beyond the astral plane lie a myriad other realities – multi-dimensional realms of love, light and joy.

In recent years, mediumship has become rather outmoded as more and more people turn to channelling. (Although people use the terms in different ways, my definition is that mediumship involves communication with 'dead' people, on the astral plane of reality – whether through telepathy, automatic writing, or trance mediumship. Channelling taps into higher planes of reality – the fifth dimension and beyond – giving us access to wise, loving beings who have either completed their physical lifetimes, or have never been physical. Many of these higher guides have come to help us make the transition to a New Age.)

As we become more aware, more conscious, we are shifting to higher frequencies, and so become able to tune into higher dimensions of reality. As we do this, we can tap into unseen friends from many different dimensions – from nature spirits to archangels, from our personal guides to the Goddess; and we can learn to work together.

In the past, it took years to train as a channel. (Some people choose to think that it still does!) However, times are changing rapidly, and human consciousness is expanding beyond the limitations of space-time. Countless people – even those with no experience of meditation – have now learnt to start channelling a high-level guide in just one weekend workshop, or by using books and tapes. As more and more of us become channels, we make it easier for others to follow in our footsteps.

Although some people are gifted as channels, my assumption is that channelling is a natural ability. Whenever we feel guided or inspired, or act upon a hunch, we are acting as channels – and many musicians, composers, artists, writers, poets, healers and therapists are channels without being aware of it. By learning to contact our unseen friends *directly*, however, we can accelerate our growth – not just because of the help and guidance they offer, but because the very process of channelling lifts and expands our consciousness.

Of course, many people still find the idea of channelling either weird or frightening. It certainly took many years before I felt comfortable with the idea – but it is worth remembering that many people were afraid of the telephone when it was first invented. (The idea of a 'disembodied voice' coming through a machine was too much to handle!) We can now communicate with others via the telephone, fax, computers, satellites, television and radio, in ways that would have seemed impossible as little as a hundred years ago. Channelling is just a wider extension of our ability to communicate – not just across the planet, but with beings in other dimensions of reality. It is a way of 'picking up the phone' to our unseen friends.

Some people are afraid of tapping into beings who might wish to 'possess' them, or give them false guidance. However, the Law is that like attracts like. If you are in a stable balanced state, and reach out with love to connect with your Higher Self or a guide, it simply isn't possible for you to attract a less evolved being. (If you did, you would know immediately – a high guide brings delicious feelings of love, warmth, humour and expansion. If you are in any doubt, just ask your Higher Self to be with you.) If a guide tries to tell you what to do, or criticises or disempowers you in any way, then I suggest that you ask for a higher guide. This is a planet of free will, and a true guide will never make your decisions for you – even if you ask them to! It is also important to remember that guides are wise friends, but they are *not* surrogate parents, *not* omniscient and *not* perfect! They are conscious beings who are on their own path of evolution.

Most people seem to have three or four guides, each with a different function. First, there is a 'guardian spirit', who is quite often a dead relative (in my case, a great grandmother). Then there is at least one 'wise one', often from an ancient culture – such as a Buddhist monk or native American Indian. (I have a shaman guide named Ikulu.) Third, there are one or more higher guides – beings of Light from higher dimensions, who can take on a human-like form when we meet them on the inner planes, or might appear as pure light.

Let me emphasise again that guides, angels and channelled sources are *conscious beings in other dimensions*. It is easy for us to overlook this miraculous fact, and dismiss guides as a comforting idea, a useful technique, an aspect of the subconscious, or 'mere imagination', rather than seeing them a wondrous reality. My greatest teachers in this lifetime have been – and continue to be – guides from other dimensions, and I never cease to feel wonder and gratitude for their presence.

If you are interested in channelling a guide directly – that is, allowing a guide to enter your aura, and speak or write through you – I highly recommend Sanaya Roman and Duane Packer's book, *Opening to Channel* (H. J. Kramer, 1987), which not only gives step-by-step instructions, but deals with all the inevitable fears, doubts and questions. I first learnt to channel my own guide, Celeste, by using their material.

However, for most people, an inner journey is the easiest and most acceptable way to contact their guide (or guides). Each time you repeat this, it strengthens the link between you, and makes it easier for your guide to contact you at other times. In time, you can learn to distinguish the different 'voices' of your guide(s), or establish ways in which they can get messages through to you. (One woman I know has a guide which has left messages on her answerphone – but guidance most often comes as an inner voice or impulse!)

MEETING YOUR GUIDE

Relax deeply, then imagine that you are on a beach. Behind you, there is a forest – and in front of you, the ocean. Allow your feet to sink into the warm sand, and slowly open your inner eyes. Notice the waves of the ocean, and the colour of the sand. Notice what time of day it is. Look at the trees behind you. Open your inner ears, hearing the crashing of the waves on the shore, the seagulls' cry, the rustling of the trees. Smell the ocean air, and taste the salt on your lips. Use all your inner senses to find yourself there . . .

Now go in search of a magical place, a place where you will meet your guide. It might be a sandy cove, or a crystal cave, or a clearing in the forest, or a stone circle. It might be an under water temple beneath the ocean waves. Or it might be a cloud in the sky. Go to wherever your heart leads you.

In this magical place, mentally ask one of your guides to join you. Wait patiently, until you see or sense someone joining you. Your guide might take a human or angelic form, or come to you as light or colour, or you might simply sense a presence, or feel a warm glow.

Welcome your guide, and ask for their name. (You might hear the name, see it, or just 'know' it. Sometimes it changes from the first name that you hear, but you'll know when you've got it right. It might well be a simple name such as Jane or Sam.) You might wish to ask whether your guide ever lived on the earth, or whether you have known each other 'before'. Or you might ask for guidance about the next steps in your life's journey, or the skills and qualities you are developing at present. Or you could ask for help in manifesting a Dream, or letting go of the past, or healing your inner Child – or whatever else you desire.

Allow this contact to be *real*. Remind yourself of the miracle of our unseen friends – and feel your gratitude towards your guide. Thank and hug your guide before saying goodbye. Return to the place on the beach where your journey began. Then slowly and gently bring yourself back into the room.

CALLING IN YOUR GUIDE

First choose a current issue or decision which you would like to receive guidance about. Relax and attune to Spirit. Then mentally call in your guide – either by name, or by asking for your 'highest guide'. For example, 'I call upon my guide Leila to help me with this issue. I am surrounded by Light, and affirm that Leila alone can enter my aura.' Then sit and wait, imagining that your guide is approaching. If you are willing, your guide will gently enter your aura. (You might feel a subtle sensation of warmth, tingling, expansion or love. Guides are usually so careful to avoid causing alarm that you are quite likely to doubt their presence, and to feel that you are 'making it up'.)

Once you sense or trust that your guide is present – it only takes a minute or two, if you are focused – think about the issue or decision. With your guide suffusing your aura, you will have a much broader perspective than usual, as if you have somehow expanded around the issue. Your thoughts will *feel* like your own, yet will be free from any fear, doubt, struggle or self-importance. (The more often you call upon your guides, the easier it becomes to tune in to their wisdom.)

A FEW WORDS ABOUT GHOSTS

When I was ten years old, my family moved to a large Victorian house which was haunted by a young woman. While practising the piano, I would often sense 'her' behind me, and hear a swish of crinoline as she turned to leave; or she would stand as a shadowy presence at the top of the stairs. On occasion, the house was electrified with her presence; at other times 'she' was absent for days or weeks at a time.

Scary though it was for a child, growing up in a haunted house was invaluable experience for me. It helped me to sense subtle shifts in energy and to open up to psychic information – and prompted my passionate interest in parapsychology and mysticism. By the age of nineteen, I was a keen ghost-hunter, visiting every haunted site I could find, and often invited by friends to 'check out' their homes.

Of course, many so-called ghosts are just rumbling water pipes, shifting foundations, reflections in a window, or sounds from a neighbour's radio. It's wise to assume that any curious sight or sound has an ordinary source, unless other explanations have been ruled out *and* there is a distinct shift in energy.

Some ghosts are psychokinetic (mind-over-matter) phenomena – typically knocks and bangs, footsteps, dislodged china and ornaments, doors opening and closing, unexplained fires or flashes of light. In this case, the action usually centres around an unhappy or psychically gifted adolescent, who creates the poltergeist without any awareness of doing so. Other hauntings are the result of intense emotions being trapped in a location, rather like a magnetic tape loop. A traumatic incident might be replayed over and over – complete with sights, sounds or smells. There is no conscious being involved; it is more like a tape recording or video of the event.

Some ghosts, however, *are* conscious beings – people who have died but haven't yet realised it, or who cannot let go and move on, perhaps because they loved their life, or always resisted change, or because they had 'unfinished business'. Most are friendly, just a little confused. They might or might not be aware of us.

Other ghosts are people we have known and loved, popping in to say hello, or to pass on a message. We might sense their presence by the sudden feeling that we are not alone, an unexplained draft of air, the clock ticking loudly, or a strange aroma. If you suspect someone is with you, just mentally say hello and welcome them. If you know who it is, do talk to them, or ask if there is any message they wish to pass on. (I have received many useful messages for other people this way – often from people I scarcely knew, but who were obviously aware that I would acknowledge their presence and listen.)

When it is the birthday of a loved one who has died, it's a lovely gesture to put a birthday card on your mantelpiece; if you send love, he or she is sure to drop in. On the other hand, do give them permission to leave you. Some souls do get stuck because their loved ones' continued grief 'holds' them close to Earth.

Then there are the living ghosts. One of my favourite ghost stories is of an American woman who dreamt regularly about a house over many years. One day, she was stunned to come across the house in 'reality', just as she had pictured it in her dreams – and it was up for sale. She knocked on the door, but the owner took one look at her and slammed the door in her face. It turned out that the house was haunted – and *she* was the ghost!

Finally, some hauntings are the result of a time warp – as if past, present and future have become folded into one another. Where there is a time warp, you might sometimes be aware of people, emotions or events in the house which are happening 'now' in another time dimension. (All time is 'really' simultaneous.) Similarly, past or future occupants of your house might be aware of you: you might be a 'ghost' yourself!

When I first moved to a lovely seventeenth-century cottage in Dorset, the atmosphere was heavy with unseen presences. It was as if the barriers between time dimensions were paper-thin, and the various inhabitants of the cottage – past, present and future – were somehow bumping into each other. My sister-in-law saw 'ghosts' in the kitchen.

Shortly after moving in, I conducted a blessing ceremony in every room with candles and small bowls of water. First I called upon Spirit, asking my guides and other unseen friends to be with me. Then I lit the first candle, affirming that only light, love and joy would abide in this room, and that the Light would spread across time, uplifting all those who lived in or passed through the house – past, present and future. The candle was lit as a symbol of the Light. Then I held the bowl of water, and flicked water into each corner of the room, affirming that any fear, anger, hurt or sadness which was being 'held' by the room would now be released. I requested that the bowl of water absorb any negativity or unresolved emotion during the night. I finished with a short Hawaiian blessing. I repeated the ceremony in every room, with a fresh candle and another bowl of water.

The next morning, I collected the bowls of water. Some were clear, others dusty or filled with granules, and others cloudy. I emptied each bowl into a rough patch of garden, asking Mother Earth to heal and transform any energy absorbed during the night, and affirming that the house could now hold nothing but love and light.

With the ceremony complete, I sat down for breakfast – and suddenly felt violently sick. A wave of sadness, grief and nausea swept through me – and I felt drawn upstairs to a small dressing room attached to the main bedroom. I already knew that a baby had died in recent years, and this had been the nursery. I blessed the room again. Minutes later, I felt terrible hurt and sadness sweeping through me, as if passing down into the earth through my feet. Emotion was being 'earthed' – and I was the conductor!

A few weeks later, a friend was staying for the weekend. Over dinner, he mentioned a couple he knew whose baby had died, and began to feel quite upset. Suddenly, there was a loud bang from upstairs. We immediately went to investigate, but could find no explanation for the noise. However, we both sensed a strong atmosphere in the 'nursery', and decided to perform an impromptu ceremony.

Tuning in, we agreed there were two 'problems': an old man from the eighteenth century who needed help in moving on, and unresolved grief from the couple who had lost their baby. Using candles, flowers, a Bible and a heartfelt desire to help, we created a loving ceremony of release. At the end, my friend felt an old, old man give him a grateful hug!

A CEREMONY OF BLESSING

(For blessing a new home, or clearing 'negative' energies or hauntings.) Gather together whatever objects feel right: perhaps candles, water, flowers, sacred texts or poetry, incense, crystals. Keep it simple, and speak from your heart. Start by attuning to Spirit, and calling in whatever unseen help feels appropriate – God/dess, Christ, your guides, power animals, spirits of the four directions, saints, angels or whoever.

Make up your own ceremony. You can't 'get it wrong', since it's your heart-felt intention that counts, not the words that you say. As an example, you might wish to light a candle, and take it to the four corners of each room: 'Let there be light where there was darkness. Let there be love where there was fear. Let there be joy in place of sadness. Let there be laughter in place of tears.' Then leave the candle burning.

Or you might wish to programme a quartz crystal to absorb any 'negative' energies over the next month, then cleanse the crystal overnight (in rock salt and spring water), then reprogramme it to magnify any light and joy in the house.

Or you might ask Spirit to help a lost soul to release the past and move on, sending the person your love, and guiding them to move towards the Light. (Doing 'rescue work' of this kind is wonderfully rewarding – though if you feel any trace of fear or doubt, it is advisable to work with friends or in a group. Even if a spirit seems to be destructive or unpleasant, I always assume that it is stuck, afraid, lost and confused, or merely childlike and playful; sometimes it is just a 'tape-loop' of unreleased emotion. I don't believe in evil spirits. As Seth said, those who believe in evil will create it.)

COMMUNICATING WITH DEVAS

Several years ago, I was walking on Dartmoor when I began to sense nature spirits all around me, dancing and celebrating. Their presence was almost tangible, and I could 'hear' their bubbling laughter. I sat on a rock, and asked whether I might see them. A laughing inner voice said, 'Stop looking with your eyes. Look with your heart.' I tried to 'see' in other ways, without success at that time – but it was good advice. In order to see or hear or feel with our inner senses, we have to learn to look, listen and touch in new, more sensitive ways.

I have yet to see a little creature with gossamer wings – which I once longed for! – but I have learnt to trust my inner senses. These days, I might 'see' a tall angelic being (as an oval of coloured light) near someone, dancing lights in their aura, the flickering light of fairies in the corner of my eye, or other signs of devic presence. Yet I suspect that almost everyone senses devas in their own way. The only difference is whether we notice and trust these impressions, or dismiss them as imagination, or a trick of the light.

The devic kingdom – the elves, gnomes, fairies, sylphs, undines, salamanders, angels, muses, archangels and so on – are part of the folklore of every culture, in varying forms. The simple explanation for this universality is that they do exist! Devas are rather like a bridge between spirit and matter. It is devas, for example, which hold the blueprint for an acorn growing into an oak tree, ensuring that it doesn't become a willow or a chrysanthemum. An apprentice deva might be responsible for a single petal of a rose, while a more evolved deva might watch over an entire forest, a species of animal or a city.

There are healing devas, ceremonial devas, landscape devas, inspirational devas, guardian devas and so on. Devas are not part of the human kingdom – although they can and do work cooperatively with us – they are on their own path of evolution. (In the Hawaiian tradition, it is said that a Conscious Self has to serve an apprenticeship as a nature spirit before becoming a Higher Self.)

Deva means 'the shining one' in Sanskrit, and when we 'see' or sense devas, they often appear as sparks of light, shimmering energy-forms or vague luminous shapes. More often, we just gain an 'impression' of their presence, which cannot be defined in terms of our usual five senses.

If you wish to 'see' nature spirits such as fairies, the usual advice is to walk in a forest or other natural landscape, and pay attention to your peripheral vision. Notice the small, flickering lights! Or just sit quietly in a garden or woodland area, and soften your gaze. De-focus slightly, so that you are not looking 'at' the scene so much as 'through' it, focusing on the spaces *in between* the plants and trees. Again, pay attention to your peripheral vision as well. (Learning to see auras, and being habitually sensitive to energy, wherever you are, also helps this process of 'tuning in' to your subtle senses.)

Communicating with devas requires attuning with Spirit – becoming calm, loving and expansive – then using whatever words feel appropriate to 'open the channel'. When I lived opposite Highgate Woods in London, I would often sit in my personal power-spot on a fallen tree trunk, and attune with the Spirit of the trees, or squirrels, or other devas – then wait receptively for a 'message' to reach me. (Usually, I feel a psychic expansion – then words come in a gentle yet powerful flow.)

One chilly winter's day, I asked the eternal question 'Who am I?' – then waited. A leaf stirred, catching my eye, and as I turned my head to look, a squirrel scampered up a tree nearby, silhouetted by a huge orange winter sun. At this moment, a voice said, 'I am the leaf that stirs in the breeze. I am the squirrel that darts round the tree. I am the tree, majestic and still. I am the winter sun as it sets. I am the jet plane that roars overhead. I am the voice that speaks, and the one who listens.'

Ever since I first visited Findhorn (the spiritual community in Scotland), and worked in their famous gardens, I wouldn't dream of transplanting a plant, tree or bush – or even pruning the roses – without briefly attuning to the devic kingdom first, and asking for their help. ('Hello, rose devas. I'm going to prune the roses now, so please help me to do so in the best possible way, so that the flowers might be bounteous and beautiful. Thank you for your help.') We can also ask the devas for inspiration before landscaping a garden – though we *are* free to ignore their wishes if we choose, and go our own way. Or we can attune to the Spirit of an ailing house or garden plant, and ask what it needs to restore its balance. (All that stands in the way is lack of faith in our natural psychic abilities.)

Similarly, if your house is invaded by ants, or your garden by moles, you can attune to the spirit of Ant or Mole, and ask them to leave. It sounds crazy, but it seems to work! Of course, it won't work if you order them to 'get off your property'. Attunement only works through the power of love. Gently explain to Ant or Mole that, although the ants or moles have as much right to live in this place as you do, you would be terribly grateful if they would move to a nearby field or patch of waste, or live in the garden rather than the house. Listen patiently for a reply (in words, images or feelings) – Ant or Mole might have another suggestion to make, or a compromise solution, such as moving out in return for having food or shelter provided. Whatever you 'hear', trust it.

As always, allow yourself to be surprised. When I moved to the country, my cat soon brought home an assortment of mice, voles, shrews and birds, which she would proceed to bat around the study with her paw in great delight – so I began to apologise to the Spirit of each animal. However, when I attuned to the Spirit of Vole one day (while my cat was chewing a fat, juicy vole outside), the matter-of-fact reply was not what I had expected: 'Waste not your grief on the creature which has passed into Spirit. When one animal hunts another, both have signed the contract. The prey is willing to change its form, and expands beyond itself as it merges with the Spirit of the hunter. It is only from your limited human perspective that cruelty and suffering are involved. As humans, you cling so tenaciously to your form! The animal kingdom knows when the time has come to move on. Everything is in balance. An agreement is made, consciousness exits the form – and the act is done. Weep not for what is.' This conversation did not stop me rescuing uninjured prey whenever I could – but it did help me to accept Gemma's hunting with far more equanimity.

POWER ANIMALS

Another form of unseen friend is the power animal. Power animals are the archetypal consciousness of a whole species. For anyone who feels superior to the animal kingdom (and most us have learnt to feel this way), working with power animals can be a humbling experience, reminding us of the wisdom of nature and the strengths of our fellow creatures. Shamans of all cultures and traditions have called upon power animals for strength, protection, balance, keen senses, empowerment and intuitive guidance.

Power animals have a reputation for turning up 'in the flesh' – often behaving in uncharacteristic ways – just to remind you that life is a dream! In one inner journey, a vulture appeared to me unexpectedly, then transformed itself into the power animal I had called upon: the turkey. A couple of weeks later, I was walking with a friend on Mount Tamilpais, the sacred mountain near San Francisco, when a bird of prey swooped down around my head. Somewhat startled,

I asked my friend what the bird was. 'It's a turkey vulture,' he replied – much to my amazement and delight. On another occasion, a mountain goat appeared on the road as we drove up a winding pass in the Canadian Rockies. It blocked our path for some time, and posed for photographs. The mountain goat was my primary power animal at the time.

At one shamanic workshop I led, I was chatting during the coffee break when two members of the group summoned me urgently into a nearby room. It was where the smokers had gathered for their fix of nicotine – and on the windowsill was an extraordinary sight. A rook stood on the sill, with a cigarette lighter in its beak. It tapped the lighter several times, then flew off with it. Apparently, the bird had flown into the room and boldly removed a small packet of tobacco. It had then returned for the lighter! (Carrion birds clear up what is no longer required, and thus often carry messages about releasing the past, or old habits.) Two of the smokers had already received 'whispers' that they should give up smoking, and decided that this guidance was too obvious to ignore!

Power animals can even be sensed by other people. One shamanic teacher, Amber Wolfe, tells of shopping in a jewellery store in New Mexico, where she was served by a native American woman.[3] The woman made it clear that she knew that Amber must be a shamanic teacher. How did she know? 'Why, the wolves walked in with you,' the woman replied. 'I saw them quite clearly!' At one of my intensive courses, I called in my primary power animal – the Wolf – and asked everyone to sense which animal it was. Four out of the eighteen people guessed the Wolf (and one said an Alsatian dog). One woman even correctly described Its grey-brown fur and amber eyes. Quite an impressive result!

Although everyone has their 'own' power animals, which are with them for life (or at least for long periods), we can call on the Spirit of any animal whose specific strengths or qualities we need. For example, I call upon Mountain Goat whenever I'm walking on narrow mountain paths, which helps me to be sure-footed.

You might wish to acquire a photograph, drawing, soft toy, wooden carving or other representation of your power animal(s). Mentally ask for your animal to come to you, then keep your eyes open – you might find it in a jumble sale, an antique shop or even lying on the ground, or it might come to you as a gift.

Your power animals mean whatever they mean to you. However, I have often found the traditional meanings of power animals useful in understanding why a particular animal has come to me. The following brief summaries are based mostly upon native American (and Celtic) traditions. (For an indispensable guide to Native American teachings, complete with a set of animal cards, see *The Medicine Cards* by Jamie Sams and David Carson, published by Bear & Co.)

MEETING YOUR POWER ANIMAL

Relax deeply, then imagine you are in a peaceful place in nature. Use all your senses to find yourself there. Then look around for a way of going deep down into the Earth: perhaps a well, a cave, a hollow tree, a mining shaft or a tunnel. Follow this passageway deep into Mother Earth until you emerge into a natural landscape: perhaps a forest, meadow, beach, desert, riverbank or mountain.

When you feel ready, call upon your power animal to join you. (You might or might not find that the landscape changes.) Before long, an animal or bird will approach you. Try not to guess what it will be – let yourself be surprised. Traditionally, the animal should present itself four times, or in four different ways, if it is your power animal. Greet the animal in a friendly and respectful way, and ask whether it is your power animal. If so, the animal might lead you on a symbolic journey, or speak to you in words about the message it carries, or the strengths or qualities which it brings as a gift.

Thank your power animal, and ask its Spirit to be with you. At this point, either the whole animal or a wispy spirit-form will merge into your body. Feel the power of the animal within you. Feel its qualities, its senses, its body within you, almost as if you are becoming that animal. Take time to absorb its energy, its Spirit. It might even give you a poem or a song. If you wish, 'become' the animal for a while – running or swimming or flying, hunting or grazing, grooming, sleeping as the animal . . . Then gently come back to the room.

(Whenever you need your power animal, just call on its Spirit, inhale deeply, and its strengths and qualities will become available to you.)

Ant

Be patient, and trust in the process of life; like the ant, work for the good of all

Antelope

Need for quick and decisive action; do it now! 'Walk your talk' – live life according to your stated beliefs

Armadillo

Be clear about your boundaries; learn to say No; also, consider whether your 'armour' has become your prison

Badger

Fight for what you want; let off steam; but beware of unhealthy expressions of anger (in self or others)

Bat

Symbolic death and rebirth; a significant change in your life, which can be painful or joyful – it's up to you! Can also be a warning about stagnation

Bear

The need to look within, and see yourself honestly; make time for silence and solitude; trust your intuition

Beaver

The builder; put your ideas into action; open new doors, and be aware of possible options; need for teamwork

Bird

Freedom; the need to free yourself, and glimpse your own potential

Blackbird

Magical secrets, and the ability to travel in the
Otherworld

Buffalo or Ox

Prayer and abundance. 'Ask and it shall be given to
you.' Be grateful for your blessings, and you will
receive

Butterfly

The need for transformation; recognise the different
stages of change – at times, it might appear that
nothing is happening; be clear about your next step;
enjoy the process rather than the goal

Cat

Focus and concentration; focus on what you
want; also useful as a guardian, and when facing
confrontation

Crow

An omen of change; need for personal integrity; know
that rules can be broken, that the only true laws are
the sacred laws; beware of rebelliousness for its own
sake; learn from and release the past

Deer

Be gentle on yourself and others; learn the power of
unconditional love and acceptance; can also help in
journeying to the Otherworld, and in shapeshifting
(see Chapter 10)

Dog

Service to humanity; be loyal to your ideals; be wary of the need for approval; learn to be your own best friend

Dolphin

Awareness, and the breath of life; breathe fully and completely; be present in the moment – and learn to play!

Dragon

A symbol of initiation, spiritual awakening; be fearless!

Eagle

Stay connected to Spirit; be aware of the spiritual lessons that you are attracting; learn to trust when venturing into new territory; also a reminder to stay in balance. (If an eagle loses a feather, it balances it by shedding a feather from the other wing)

Eel

Useful as a protector; also offers wisdom and inspiration

Elk

Pace yourself to avoid burnout; beware of increasing stress; seek support from friends of your own gender

Fox

The ability to be unseen; observe others without being noticed; stand back and watch for a while

Frog

Need to cleanse or refresh yourself; clear any negativity from your environment; perhaps you need a short retreat before 'taking the plunge'

Hare

Bringer of intuitive messages from the Otherworld

Hawk

Be alert for a message; observe carefully. Hawk also gives access to the wisdom of the ages

Horse

A symbol of power and compassion; the need for balance and wholeness; wisdom comes from remembering your whole journey; the horse is also a helpful guide in the Otherworld

Horse – winged

Inspiration; reach for the stars!

Hummingbird

Spread joy, beauty and magic in the world! Be aware of your need for freedom; keep an open heart

Jaguar

Magical animal often associated with the call to become a shaman

Lion

Be wary of the abuse of power, whether you are leading or being led; lead with integrity; be lion-hearted

Lizard

Be clear about your Dreams for the future – and work towards manifesting them; also, pay attention to your dreams at night

Lynx

Someone might be hiding something from you; trust your intuition; consult oracles; beware of gossiping

Moose

Have pride in a job well done; be aware of the difference between healthy self-esteem and egotism

Mouse

Pay attention to detail; get yourself organised; observe yourself and others closely

Otter

Faithfulness, compassion and sharing; protection and healing; honour and value your feminine side; don't take life too seriously

Owl

Beware of deception; be discerning; be honest with yourself

Ox

See *Buffalo*

Pig

Creative inspiration, clairvoyance and prophecy

Porcupine

The need for childlike faith, trust and innocence

Rabbit

Don't be so fearful; what you resist will persist; relax, nurture yourself, and release your fears

Raven

Magic is in the air – perhaps a shift in consciousness? Be willing to face your own darkness; beware of wishing harm to anyone. (Raven is also the power animal for England)

Reindeer

The gift of knowledge; joyfulness in knowledge and wisdom

Salmon

The acquisition of knowledge; the healing of emotional wounds; go with the flow

Skunk

The need for self-respect and quiet authority; be wary of leaking energy to others

Snake

The need for change, and to 'shed your old skin'; accept every aspect of your life if you wish to change

Spider

Be aware that you weave your own web, and don't get trapped in your own illusion; also release your creativity; perhaps keep a journal?

Squirrel

Prepare for the future, and release anything which

no longer serves you; don't cling to the past through fear

Stag

The power of the 'masculine' within us; can also help in journeying to the Otherworld, and in shapeshifting

Swan

Trust and surrender to the process of life; trust your intuition, and go with the flow

Turkey

The need to transcend self to serve others; be generous with your spirit; don't give in order to receive

Turtle

Honour Mother Earth and the Goddess; stay grounded

Unicorn

Bring magic into your life; don't waste time

Whale

Listen to the whispers; you have all the answers within; psychic powers and clairaudience

Wolf

Wisdom; an innovator who has come to teach; everything is your teacher; keep seeking new teachers; spend time in lonely power spots

Woodpecker

A symbol of wealth

THE POWER OF THE GODDESS

The gods and goddesses of ancient cultures might be seen as archetypal energies, or as conscious beings from the angelic realms, who have passed into our collective unconscious. (Just as the Judaeo-Christian tradition has its angels and archangels, other cultures have their gods and goddesses.) Either way, we can ask for their help in the same way that we might call upon our guides or power animals.

Most Westerners are familiar with the Greek and Roman gods and goddesses, archangels such as Michael and Gabriel, and less often with the Celtic deities such as Ceridwen and Rhiannon. The goddesses of Hawaii are much less well-known, but I have found them powerful energies to work with:

Hina

The goddess of beauty. Hina is the most well-known goddess in Polynesia, representing the feminine principle, the moon and the sea. She dresses in silver and white. We can invoke her when we wish our inner beauty to shine through, to help us live in harmony with our emotions and body, or whenever we need to 'be' more and 'do' less.

Haumea

The goddess of childbirth and abundance. Her name means The Builder, and she is an Earth-mother goddess, linked with the mineral kingdom. Invoke her for fertility and childbirth, or to attract prosperity and abundance.

Hi'iaka

The goddess of action. Hi'iaka was known for her adventures, overcoming evil dragons and bringing her lover back from the dead. Invoke her for healing, for awareness and for courage.

Pele

The goddess of energy. Pele is the fiery goddess of volcanoes. Her name means The Mover, and her element is fire. She can be invoked for energy, passion and motivation.

Laka

The goddess of love. Laka is associated with fragrances and plants – useful for aromatherapists and herbalists. Her name means The Attracter, and she dresses in green. Laka can be invoked when we wish to attract love and friendship.

Kapo

The goddess of dreams. Her name means The Unseen One, and she carries the powers of psychic abilities and working with dreams.

Uli

The goddess of magic. Dressed in deep purple or dark clothing. Invoke her when you wish to manifest a Dream, or need help in understanding a message or guidance.

When you wish to invoke a goddess, attune to Spirit, then imagine that you are in a beautiful landscape. When you are ready, call upon the goddess, using whatever words feel appropriate. For example, 'I call upon the goddess Hi'iaka. Please help me find the courage to move towards my Dreams, to take the steps that are necessary, and to hold a clear vision of the future.' Then wait expectantly until the goddess arrives. She might appear in human or angelic form, or might be swirling energy, or a ball of light, or you might just sense Her presence around you. The goddess might give you healing energy, or inspire you with new ideas, or you might not know what is happening, yet sense that She is doing whatever is necessary. (If you prefer, invoke the goddess without any visualisation, allowing her to come to you where you sit. You might sense Her as energy, or hear Her words as thoughts in your head.)

Once you have worked with the Hawaiian goddesses for a while – or with any other representatives of the feminine principle – you might wish to invoke the Goddess Herself. If so, take it seriously. Take a bath or shower, light candles and incense, and ask Her to come to you in whatever form She wishes to take. (She might come to you as a vision, as energy, as words, as sensation, or as an urge to rebalance your life and express more of your 'feminine' side.) Just sit quietly, and wait . . . Repeat the process until you have an unmistakably powerful experience of the presence and love of the Goddess.

We are not alone. We live in a loving universe, and are surrounded by unseen helpers. *All we have to do is ask*. If you are programming your future, ask for help in co-creating it. If you need guidance, ask for it. If you need healing, ask for it. If you need peace of mind, or courage, or a sense of humour, ask for it. If you wish to bless a house, ask for help. Ask your guides, ask the angels, ask channelled sources, ask the nature spirits, ask your power animals, ask a saint, ask the archangels, ask God/dess. 'Ask!' says Orin. 'We cannot give you anything unless you ask. The universe waits for you to ask.'[4]

And if you should ever feel lonely or afraid or upset – or perhaps when you are overflowing with love, joy and gratitude – just close your eyes, reach out your hand, and sense the gentle squeeze as an unseen friend places their reassuring hand in yours.

8

Many Hands, Light Work

*Our power lies in our clarity about the role our work
can play in the creation of a more beautiful world.
The miracle is to think of our career as our contribution, however small, to the healing of the universe.*

(Marianne Williamson[1])

'Thank God it's Friday!' The Old Age view is that
work is just a means of earning a living. It pays the
bills, keeps a roof over our head, gives us an identity and makes us feel useful. It is probably monot-
onous, tiring and soul-less, and we have to do it for
forty years or so – but if we're lucky, we get an annual
holiday so that we can lie on the beach for two weeks,
and gather the strength to face another year. In any
case, there's always retirement to look forward to!

In the New Age, our attitudes towards work are
changing dramatically. We are reclaiming the fun, the
joy, the passion of work. We are learning to do what
we love, to follow our hearts – because in doing so,
we are putting Spirit back into our work. We are
remembering what we came here to do – our sacred
Dream, the unique contribution we came to make,
the way in which we will 'breathe out' to the world.

Whatever you most want to do, whatever your
heart longs for, whatever feels most challenging and

makes your adrenaline flow with excitement, or allows hours to pass like minutes – this is what you have come to do.

Your life's work won't reveal itself in a blinding flash of light. You won't wake up one morning knowing that your task is to found an educational charity which will preserve the knowledge and wisdom of tribal peoples, or to develop vehicles which run on water and sunlight. Instead, you might be drawn into running and organising evening classes, and fund-raising for charity, then take a trip to Thailand and become fascinated by the culture of the hilltribes – and so it goes on. Or you might train in engineering and technology, gain experience in transport, then become involved in environmental pressure groups. Slowly, you move towards combining your areas of expertise. Step by step, our sacred Dream unfolds. All we need to know is the next step to take.

Our uniqueness is our gift to the world. No two people have the same qualities, vision and experience, and our life's work emerges from our own individual melting pot. Usually, it is only in retrospect that we can see why we completed a certain training course, or worked for a given charity, or developed a particular hobby. Experience is never wasted, and looking at where we have been offers clues as to where we are going.

Often, it is when we *combine* various skills or interests that we discover our life's work – and a long-standing hobby might suddenly fit into the jigsaw puzzle. I've enjoyed singing all my life, and used to yearn for singing lessons – but my workaholic side told me it would be a waste of time and money, since it was 'just for fun'. In my early thirties, I found a singing teacher at last, and it soon became clear why I needed to develop my voice: to project my voice in large lecture halls, and to lead chanting and cere-mony in workshops. Nothing is ever wasted, and whatever we long from our hearts to do – however humble, however grand – is guidance from Spirit.

DISCOVERING YOUR LIFE'S WORK

1. Write down all of your work experience so far (including unpaid and voluntary work). What have you learnt from each of these jobs? What knowledge, skills and abilities have you gained? What are your personal strengths? What are your 'natural talents'? What other resources do you have (e.g. capital, spare outbuildings, business/personal contacts)? What are your hobbies and interests (past and present)? What brings you most joy? Finally, write down the global Dream(s) which excite you most – how you most want to see the world change. If you stir all of these ingredients together, you will find many clues about the essence of your life's work.

(Sometimes our work experience is complementary. For example, you might work in a bank for ten years to get your feet on the ground, and learn the skills of money management, before developing your psychic or healing abilities – although you would have had various 'pointers' towards your future career. Most of us do not begin our life's work until our mid-30s, and some – needing a whole range of skills and experience – start much later than this.)

2. Attune to Spirit, and ask for a symbol of your life's work. Wait patiently until you receive an image of some kind – and send thanks to Spirit. Then draw, make or buy the image that you saw, and put it where you will see it every day. Each time you look at it, mentally ask Spirit to show you the next step towards your life's work – and 'know' that the guidance will come to you. (Wild Oat, the Bach Flower remedy, can also be useful in awakening to your life purpose.)

Some years ago, when I asked Spirit for a symbol of my life's work, I was shown – on several occasions – the image of two serpents winding up the staff of Hermes, the messenger god. It was only much later that I realised how appropriate this was. Not only is it a symbol of healing; it also represents the blending of two worlds, the staff which links heaven and Earth – the 'sacred marriage' of our left and right side.

DOING WHAT YOU LOVE

'Skill is not the answer, neither is money. What you need is optimism, humanism, enthusiasm, intuition, curiosity, love, humour, magic and fun and that secret ingredient – euphoria' (Anita Roddick, founder of the Body Shop)[2].

Many people believe that they cannot do what they

love *and* pay the bills. Sometimes, this is because they haven't yet discovered how to *combine* their various skills and interests to offer something unique to the world. Sandie was trained as a Gestalt psychotherapist, but most of all she loved to dance. She now runs workshops in dance and movement as a tool for personal growth. Tony was skilled as a carpenter, and also a keen guitar and mandolin player. He set up a successful business making musical instruments to order. Sometimes we need to combine our skills and talents with others (or to change our business partner). Julia was a teacher of English literature, whose great passion was travelling. She married Ian, whose background was in theology and mysticism. Together, they now organise and lead 'sacred tours' all over the world – and supplement their income by writing about their travels.

Another common reason for feeling frustrated or stuck is believing that work is *supposed* to be a struggle! If you find that you only earn money while doing something that you dislike, or that your friends and family complain about their jobs, then you need to explore your beliefs about work. If so, create a spider chart – see Chapter 4 – and write 'Work is . . .' in the centre of the circle. Write down whatever thoughts, beliefs or messages come to mind. Then change any negative beliefs – and look at your payoffs for clinging to work that you dislike. (Martyrhood? Approval-seeking? Staying safe? Preferring daydreams to action?)

As the New Age approaches, it is becoming much easier to create prosperity if we are doing what we love. As the Earth plane shifts to a higher frequency, many of those who work purely for money are being made redundant, or finding their profits begin to tumble so that they are *forced* to change. It is becoming more and more crucial to do what we love.

'But who will do all the boring, mundane jobs?' My assumption is that soul-destroying jobs will gradually disappear when people are no longer prepared to do them. We will find new solutions, new ways of getting tasks done, if there is sufficient will to do so. Also, we should not assume that everyone finds the same jobs dull! I used to have a cleaner who bubbled with enthusiasm about her work, and counted herself very lucky. She felt sorry for me, as I spent hours sitting at a computer screen each day. It's all a question of attitude – and finding the job that is right *for you*.

'But what if I make the wrong choice?' Before entering this lifetime, your soul decided upon the *essence* of your life's work, your chosen destiny. The *form* that it takes is up to you. There are no wrong choices. Your Higher Self does not have a tablet of stone inscribed with your life assignment: 'Write twenty novels and sixty short stories on the theme of the healing power of love. Do not return Home until this mission is completed.' This isn't how Spirit operates!

Writing novels is a chosen form, not the essence. If your chosen themes are, say, 'the healing power of love' and 'communication/teaching', then your life's work *might* take the form of being a novelist – or you might be a doctor in a teaching hospital, or a management consultant who helps businesses to 'live with heart', or you might run a children's home, or be a garage mechanic, or a thousand other possibilities. If you enjoy what you do, then you are in the right job (at least for the moment).

When we are on our highest path, doors tend to open easily. It is easy to create success – even 'miracles' – if we act in harmony with our chosen destiny. (When I began freelance writing, at the age of 21, almost every article I wrote was accepted by the top women's magazines – and I was quickly offered a regular contract. Looking back, I can see that this was Spirit's way of encouraging me to keep writing, since it was crucial to my life's work.)

If you are struggling to get work, or doors keep slamming in your face, then you might be running up a blind alley, or perhaps your timing is wrong. If you do make a choice that doesn't work out, try something else! You will have gained from the experience – and at least you tried. There are no mistakes – only learning.

If the job you want does not yet exist, then why not create it? Steve, the Loch Ness monster hunter (Chapter 4), did not sit around waiting for a post as 'monster hunter' to be advertised. He just went ahead and created it!

Another approach is to write down the essence of your ideal job. For example: 'Flexible hours, work with my hands, travel, healing, music, work with people, keep learning, organise, be creative . . .' Then attune to Spirit, light a candle, and burn the paper, asking Spirit to send your ideal job, or to show you the next step towards it. (Keep a copy of your list, so that you can look back in amazement when you have found the job of your Dreams!) Or you can take an inner journey to meet your Future Self, and ask it for guidance.

If you have no idea what your heart longs to do, then spend time in a reference library, or visit a good careers advisor, or just try something – anything! – until you discover what sets you alight with enthusiasm. Or take an inner journey to meet the self which is blocking you from knowing what you want; listen to its fears, give it love, and clear the blockage. In the words of Ralph Waldo Emerson, *whatever* work you do in the meantime, 'put your love where your labour is'. When we love what we are doing, we are much more magnetic to our ideal job.

ARE YOU IN THE RIGHT JOB?

1. What do you enjoy? Tick whichever apply from the list below. Give two ticks to any items which are a high priority for you. (Feel free to add your own ideas.)

Being creative/innovative
Coming up with new ideas
Meeting new people
Working as part of a team
Being independent
Having to make quick
  decisions
Having deadlines to meet
Regular, guaranteed income
Research/statistics
Managing/leading others
Having a finished product
Having an office to go to
Getting the details right
Putting ideas on paper
Working on projects
Working at home
Keeping accounts

Marketing/selling
Money management
Healing
Working with animals
Working with plants
Being outdoors/in nature
Travelling
Taking risks
Singing/dancing/theatre
Using your imagination
Speaking on telephone
Fundraising
Making/building things
Working with mass media
Working on computers
Putting ideas into practice
Inspiring people
Having a business partner(s)

Creating a vision of the future	Committee work
Helping people one-to-one	Co-ordinating groups
Reaching large numbers of people	Simplifying complex data
Writing	Doing something new
Teaching	Reading
Negotiating	Having an impact on institutions
Feeling challenged	Problem-solving
Working with people in need	Lots of variety
New Age ideas	Lots of free time
Living in city	Working with children
Living in countryside	Working regular hours
Having a steady routine	Working flexible hours
Being physically active	Caring for others
Inner work/meditation	Being playful
Art and crafts	Networking
Working with your hands	Busy, hectic workplace
Helping people find solutions	Working in peace and quiet
	Running your own business

2. Does your current job offer the opportunities, challenges and working environment that you have ticked? Could you shift the emphasis in your current job so that it *does* offer what you want? Or do you need to change your line of work? (Don't assume that you're in the wrong job just because you have no like-minded people around you. Your task might be as a Light-keeper in that company or institution, if that is a role you enjoy.)

3. If you could do anything you wanted, without any financial worries, what would you do? What would your ideal lifestyle be? How could you move towards this lifestyle *now*?

4. What does success mean *to you*? (Try to ignore what it means to other people. Ask yourself what it means to *you*.

'YES BUT . . .' AND 'WHAT IF . . .'

Everyone has inner gremlins which trip us up, just as we start to feel hopeful and courageous. What are your favourite excuses for not doing what you love? Do you play the 'yes but' game? ('Yes, but I'm not clever enough/talented enough/rich enough/well-qualified enough . . .' 'Yes, but we're in a recession.' 'Yes, but I'm a single parent.' 'Yes, but no one would pay me to do what I love.' 'Yes, but it would mean a drop in income.' 'Yes, but most people dislike their jobs, so it's OK if I do.')

Or perhaps you prefer the 'what if game? ('What if I fail?' 'What if I run out of money?' 'What if the house falls down?') Or perhaps you procrastinate? ('I'll do that course *next* year.' 'I'll start when the children leave home.' 'I'll change when I'm 30/40/50.') Or do you use ambivalence as an excuse? ('One day I want to go for it, the next day I don't – so I guess I'm just not ready yet.') Or is money your excuse? ('I'd do it if I had the money, but I'll just have to wait.')

Whatever our resistance, we pay a heavy price for it. It blocks us from our joy and aliveness. It blocks us from our sacred Dream. It blocks us from our Higher Self. It can mean a wasted lifetime. (Yes, you can have plenty more lives, but are you really prepared to waste *this* life – a lifetime for which your Higher Self has such high hopes, a lifetime in which you have boundless opportunities?)

Whenever we follow our hearts, Spirit jumps for joy, and usually lends a helping hand. When I resigned from my job in the Health Service, I had minimal savings and a large mortgage. I had no plans other than to write *Living Magically*, plus some vague notions about freelance writing and teaching, but I 'knew' beyond all doubt that I was making the right decision. I trusted that I would be led, step by step, towards my higher purpose. It felt very much like stepping off a cliff – scary but exhilarating! Since then, I have lived my Dreams more and more. Have I ever regretted my decision to leave my secure job? Not for a single moment!

THE IMPORTANCE OF 'MOODLING'

Whatever your job – whether you're a homoeopath, a systems analyst, a housewife or a market gardener – the most important time in your working week is (or should be) your 'ideas time'. Being creative and innovative in our work makes it challenging and fulfilling, and helps us grow through joy rather than struggle. When I worked in the Health Service, I regularly slotted an 'ideas session' into my diary – which meant reviewing how I spent my time, which aspects of work excited me most, how I could improve my working practices or use time more effectively, as well as brainstorming new ways of approaching community mental health.

Depending upon your job, you might wish to use your 'ideas session' to consider innovative ways of marketing or publicising your work, new services you might offer, reviewing your priorities, reorganising your time, how to expand, how to inject more fun or more challenge into your work, or how to resolve a problem which is bugging you. Or you might decide to change your job, start a new career or take a training course. Regular 'ideas sessions' offer an opportunity to tap into your left side, and listen to the whispers from Spirit.

For each ideas session, you might take a notepad and pen into a nearby park, or a church, or the garden, or a quiet space where you will not be disturbed. Notice when and where you feel most inspired. (If your best ideas come to you in the bath, or on long country walks, then treat those times in your week as top priority – and make sure your notepad is always to hand.) Attune to Spirit, then ask for inspiration about (say) what you should change in your work, or projects and ideas for the future, or how to make your work more effective or more joyful.

Write down any ideas which give you a buzz, even if they sound outrageous. The 'crazy' or quirky ideas are often the best! (I once came across a jaded city solicitor who had decided to become a landscape artist – despite the fact that she hadn't touched a paint-brush since she was at school! Within two years, she was earning a small but adequate living as an artist, and moved to a rural idyll in Wales.)

After your ideas session, review your notes, decide which ideas to follow up, and commit yourself to action (e.g. 'Phone Susan and Tom tomorrow to discuss new proposal.' 'Make enquiries about evening classes in furniture renovation.' 'Contact local radio re publicity idea.') Make sure you act immediately, before your gremlins have time to gather their wits and offer resistance!

Many of us grew up with a puritanical, nose-to-the-grindstone view of what 'work' is, but my experience is that I work best when my life is in balance, and I take plenty of long country walks. If I get lost in busy-ness, I rarely use my time well, and almost never come up with new ideas. Our receptive, listening (left side) time is of equal importance to our active, productive (right side) time.

Brenda Ueland points out that inspiration comes slowly and quietly, and needs what she calls 'moodling' – generous times of dreamy idleness, pottering and dawdling. 'These people who are always briskly doing something and as busy as waltzing mice, they have little, sharp, staccato ideas,' she says, 'but they have no slow, big ideas.'[3] When we dash about, always active, we are limited to our right side.

Mahatma Gandhi used to spin his own cloth, which I'm sure – apart from its political significance – was an opportunity for moodling. *Your* moodling time might involve lying in bed, going for walks, decorating the house, playing cricket, travelling, gardening, watching soap operas on TV ... Of course, only *you* can know whether such activities mean that you are moodling – making space for your left side – or whether you are just fretting, worrying, feeling muggy, wasting time or avoiding what needs to be done.

Workaholics are very disdainful of moodling. They're much too busy for such 'luxuries'. The workaholic is fearful, inadequate and driven, with desperation lurking just beneath the surface. Work is an escape rather than a joy. Those who truly *love* their work, on the other hand, are joyful, open, playful, seemingly unhurried yet passionate, can stop work and relax at any time – and they *adore* moodling!

GIVING BIRTH TO A PROJECT

Whenever we create something new – whether it is a business, a book, a brochure, a project report, a painting or a dress design – it is important to devote time to inner work, so that we give birth to the project in its highest form. If we skip this stage, the result can be muddled, chaotic and unsatisfying.

Inner work can take various forms – such as allowing time for 'moodling', processing and programming the future, transforming any blockages, or just waiting for the right time. It can also include 'working with the project as energy'.

Everything that will ever exist already has an unmanifest energy pattern. The energy pattern might be dark and messy, full of clashing colours, bright and harmonious, ordered and symmetrical, or chaotic but interesting – and each pattern would have a different 'form' when translated into physical reality. By working with the energy pattern of a project before we translate it into physical reality, we can produce what we want in the highest possible form, and with far greater ease than if we rushed straight into it.

Whenever I sit down to prepare a brochure, or plan a workshop, or write an article, I start by working with the project as energy, and 'birthing it into matter' – a technique I first learnt from Orin and DaBen.[4]

WORKING WITH A PROJECT
AS ENERGY

Relax deeply, then imagine that somewhere in
the distance is the project in its unmanifest
form, as an energy pattern. (If you haven't
given much thought to the project, this 'form' is
likely to be rather vague or dark or chaotic. If
it's an important project which you have been
mulling over for a while, its energy form might
be more brilliant, exciting or intriguing.)

Send out your consciousness as if you're
'looking' for the project. Perhaps it is a swirling
cloud of blue-grey mist, or a moving geometric
of coloured triangles, or tiny explosions of
coloured light, or a pulsing violet and orange
sphere. Once you can see or sense it, imagine
this pattern becoming more beautiful, dazzling,
harmonious or interesting. Fill it with love and
joy. Use your consciousness to change the
energy pattern until it feels finished.

The next step is to bring it into physical reality.
Imagine that there is a barrier between you and
the energy pattern, which marks the boundary
between physical and non-physical realities.
(Non-physical realities are simply vibrating at a
different frequency.) Mentally pull the energy
pattern through the barrier, thus 'birthing it into
matter'. You might see this as a pile of snowflakes
coming in through an open attic window, or
through a door suspended in space, or an almost
invisible spider's web, or in any form you choose.

Once birthed into matter, imagine that the energy pattern is slowly approaching, still magnetising it towards you. It passes into your auric field, and into your thoughts and emotions, then into your physical body. Then ask for your cells to absorb the energy into your DNA.

(This process is much simpler than it sounds. Once you get the hang of it, it need only take a few minutes – and starting the project itself is surprisingly easy after this preparatory work.)

MAGNETISING CLIENTS/ CUSTOMERS/OPPORTUNITIES

(For those who are self-employed, working in business or in need of new contacts or opportunities in their work.)

Relax deeply, then imagine you are on a deserted beach. Use all of your inner senses to find yourself on the beach. Then look around for some means of flying – perhaps a huge kite, a pair of wings, a helicopter, an eagle or your guide. You are going to fly across the sea to a distant mountain with a magnificent temple on top.

Fly towards the mountain, and circle high above the temple. Notice a huge open courtyard, and gently come down to land in it. Your guide (or your Higher Self) will now welcome you, and lead you to the centre of the courtyard.

Tell your guide what you see as the higher purpose(s) of your work. How does (or will) your work serve people? How will it help to create a better world? Tell your guide about your vision of the future, and why you passionately believe in your work. Then ask your guide to help you in magnetising clients or contacts for your work or new opportunities.

Imagine beams of light emerging from your heart, and mentally call clients or contacts towards you. These beams of light are now magnetising people who share your vision, or who would benefit from your work. See people entering the courtyard, and beginning to surround you. Imagine more and more people filling the courtyard. Do you feel comfortable about attracting as many people as this towards your work? Keep magnetising until you feel there are enough people. (You might need two or three contacts, or several thousand.) Tell these people how you hope to serve or work with them.

Finally, ask your guide whether there is any further action you need to take, so that these clients or contacts are aware of your work. Thank your guide, thank your future clients or contacts – and gently come back to the room. Repeat as often as you like.

A gentle warning: this process can be very powerful, so be prepared to get what you are asking for! (This inner journey is available on my *Creating Success in Business* CDs.)

A FEW WORDS ABOUT MONEY

Traditionally, those on the spiritual Path have distinguished between material and spiritual goals – but this assumes there is a split between matter and spirit. If everything is a spark of the creative Source, then a pumpkin is as spiritual as a priest, a credit card is as spiritual as a candle. Every Dream is a spiritual Dream. God/dess is *everything*!

Money is simply an energy which mirrors our beliefs about the abundance of the universe, and how 'deserving' we feel. There is not a fixed amount of money in the world. As any economist will confirm, money magically expands and contracts, according to people's confidence levels. When we collectively feel positive and abundant, the economy is buoyant. When we collectively feel fearful and limited, the economy sinks.

Does this mean it is more spiritual to be rich? Of course not. But neither is it more spiritual to be poor! If it were, why would we be so concerned about world poverty? On the contrary, poverty blocks our spiritual growth, since it means we have to focus on mere survival.

Money is certainly not a panacea; it does not guarantee happiness or love or security; but it is a form of empowerment. Unless we decide to live in a monastery or convent for the rest of our lives, we need money to live – and even more money if we are to grow and change, and give Light to the world! And although earning money is only *one* way of receiving it, it is the usual method for most of us. It is also a symbol of how much we value ourselves, how much we think we are worth, how much responsibility we take for our lives, and how much power we can allow ourselves.

The joy is that the more money we create, the more we have to give. Every time I spend money, I remind myself that I am contributing to someone else's prosperity – and imagine what a joy it would be to write huge cheques for your favourite charities, to give unexpected gifts to your friends, or be able to make others' Dreams come true! Money in itself is a meaningless goal – but creating money *in order* to create our personal and global Dreams, *in order* to fulfil our life's work, is essential to our higher purpose.

We need to abandon the Old Age idea that money is somehow 'bad', that it is more spiritual to be self-denying, puritanical martyrs. As we move into the New Age, it is time to open up to limitlessness and abundance. It is time to live our Dreams, and help others to live theirs. Money – like joy, or love, or courage – is just an energy. We can open up to that boundless energy, allowing it to flow freely in and out of our lives, or we can block it. The choice is ours.

As we *bless* those who are prosperous, rather than judging or envying them, we attract prosperity into our own lives, so that we too can create our Dreams, fulfil our higher purpose, and live easily and happily in the world.

GREEN ISSUES AND SPIRITUALITY

What about environmental issues? The planet does not have unlimited resources. We are fast depleting our rainforests, the ozone layer, fossil fuels and other natural resources – so where does abundance thinking come in?

As I understand it, we have created ecological problems *in order to find the solutions*. Environmental issues are forcing us to think globally, to widen our perspective, to work together as nations, and to recognise that we are not separate from each other, or from our planet. The ecological crisis is an opportunity to recognise that we cannot take from the planet without giving back, and that we must choose between a doom-and-gloom scenario of following the dinosaurs into extinction, or a vision of a New Age in which we work together globally to create a safe, clean, peaceful and harmonious planet for future generations.

Every global issue is a mirror of issues we are facing collectively – and points the way towards possible solutions. Our dependence on fossil fuels, for example, mirrors our belief that 'supplies will run out one day', that there is not enough to go round, and our tendency to cling to the past. As we release our scarcity beliefs, think more abundantly and hold a new vision of the future, we will create ways of using clean, safe, renewable and limitless sources of energy.

So – if we recycle our bottles, re-use envelopes and switch off unnecessary lights, are we giving in to scarcity beliefs, or perhaps just being self-righteous? Only you can know. For many people, recycling and conserving resources is a joyful aspect of caring for our planet, and a metaphor for bringing what is *useful* from the past into the present. It can make us more aware of our connectedness with the planet and mineral kingdoms, and Mother Earth herself. For other people, their motives for recycling might be a little more dodgy!

I have my doubts about whether re-using glass bottles is going to save the planet – but it is the impact on our *consciousness*, on our *awareness*, of using a bottle bank that really matters. It is the way in which that consciousness spills over into loving others, loving the world, in every aspect of our lives. It is the difference between apathy and detachment, or caring and connectedness. Now *that* can transform our planet.

PERSONAL CHANGE, GLOBAL CHANGE

I believe that our first responsibility is to make our own lives work. By finding inner peace, for example, we *are* contributing towards global peace – far more effectively than someone who waves banners and writes protest letters while feeling embattled within themselves. World peace begins with inner peace. (Once we have found inner peace, we might choose to approach the issue of world peace from a higher perspective – and therefore have a far greater impact.)

Intuitively, I believe that socio-political action which is motivated by fear, resentment, 'noblesse oblige', self-righteousness, low self-esteem or avoiding issues in one's personal life, is unlikely to have a positive impact. Born of fear, it will not have the energy to transform. Similarly, I suspect that money which is given to charity from guilt, or the desire to feel 'better than', is the same money which leaks out into administrative costs, or fails to reach its intended target.

Whatever global issue concerns you, it is worth asking yourself what the issue symbolises for you *personally*, and how you can contribute by changing yourself. If you are involved in women's issues, is your own 'feminine' and 'masculine' energy well-balanced and integrated; have you resolved your relationship with your own father? If you are concerned about the ozone layer, are you feeling unprotected in your life, or unsure of your own boundaries? If you are troubled by child abuse, are you caring for your own inner Child, or does the issue give you an opportunity to release your suppressed anger or sadness? If your heart goes out to 'prisoners of conscience', in what ways do you prevent yourself being free? This is not to say that the global issues are not important in their own right. They certainly are. It is just that we have *also* created them as symbols – both personally and globally.

Inner and outer constantly mirror each other. They are two sides of the same coin. Socio-political action must go hand-in-hand with personal growth, with self-awareness – but it *is* healing at a personal level to be involved in social, environmental and global issues, in however small a way. Social action can help to heal our inner wounds. As we reach out with love towards the world – perhaps through our paid work, and/ or by helping out at a charity shop, writing letters on behalf of Amnesty International, sponsoring a child in the Third World, working as a Samaritan, recycling our cans and bottles, buying only free-range eggs, purchasing an acre of rainforest, setting up a group or project, or whatever we feel moved to do – it reminds us of our connectedness. It helps us to expand beyond our limited right side, our separateness, and remember that we are all One.

Of course, taking outer action is only one way of

serving the world. We can also help – far more than we might imagine – by working on the inner planes. By holding a vision of the future we wish to create, or sending love and healing to those who need it, we can have a powerful impact on the world. (If we work with friends or in groups, the results can be even more dramatic.)

For example, many people have been working on the inner planes to prevent a major earthquake in California – by 'filling' the San Andreas fault with love, or holding a vision of San Francisco or LA in the twenty-first or twenty-second century, or by communicating with the Earth herself. (This only sounds crazy if we forget that everything is conscious energy, and that we create our own reality.) Is it a coincidence that the severe San Francisco earthquake of 1989 claimed astonishingly few lives, quite against the odds?

HEALING THE PLANET

There is no right or wrong way to work on the inner planes. It is our intention which counts. If you put your heart and soul into sending love and light to famine-struck areas, or to homeless people, or to the dolphins, or to a disaster zone, or to a global problem, or to a country which needs more Light, then that energy will go where it is needed, regardless of what 'technique' you use.

First, attune to Spirit. Then you might choose to send light, or colour, or feel love in your heart, or joyfully visualise the future you wish to create, or pray to Spirit for help. All that matters is the love that you feel, and your intention to heal. Trust that you will know when it is time to stop; it might be after two minutes, or twenty minutes.

(You might start or end each day with global healing – or make it a weekly or fortnightly session. If you're not good at regular commitments, just send healing whenever you feel like it. Once a year is better than never!)

MANY HANDS, LIGHT WORK

Although our Ego might fondly imagine that we are here to save the planet, or at least to do something grand and impressive, the reality is that – with the exception of rare inspirational leaders like Mother Theresa and Martin Luther King – we are here to offer our own *small* contribution to the world. As individuals, our task is not an onerous one. We simply have to light our own candle: to live with joy, to live in harmony, to do what we love, and reach for our Dreams. As each of us begins to live in the Light, the world becomes a brighter and brighter place to live.

Changing our world is a collective labour of love. Each of us is a unique piece in the giant jigsaw puzzle of life – and as everyone plays their own part in increasing the light, love and joy on our planet, we will co-create a New Age. There are thousands upon thousands of Light-keepers alive on the planet today, and many more are being born to continue our work for future generations. We are also constantly inspired and guided by our unseen friends. We are not alone in our visions, in our hopes. Together, step by step, we can *and will* create a heaven on Earth.

Magic Moments

The clouds above us join and separate,
The breeze in the courtyard leaves and returns,
Life is like that, so why not relax?
Who can stop us from celebrating?

(Lu Yu[1])

I remember once gazing at the steam rising from a coffee mug, my heart filled with inexplicable joy and wonder at the beauty and majesty of this 'ordinary' event. Yet how often do we fully see and hear and touch and feel the ordinary miracle of our everyday lives? How often are we 'too busy' even to watch the sun set, or listen to the birds sing? How often do we treat today as 'just another day'? How much of our precious lives do we waste in gentle slumbering?

In Hawaiian, the word 'ano' means present moment, seed, peaceful, awe, holy and sacred. In English, it is no coincidence that the word 'present' also means 'a gift'. The present moment is a sacred gift – and unless we are fully 'present' in this moment, we are not fully alive. The Buddhist teacher Thich Nhat Hanh notes that to live without awareness – for example, to drink tea without *knowing* that we are drinking tea – is to live as a dead person. 'Time is not money. Time is much more precious than money.

Time is life,' I once heard him say. 'Spend your time drinking your tea!'[2]

The present moment is our point of power. Now is the only time we can live. Now is the only time that we can change, release the past or make decisions. The more 'present' we are in any experience, the more we gain from it. It is rare to have any problems *now*, in this moment – unless a mad dog is ravaging you, or a bailiff is throwing your possessions on to the street. The vast majority of stress comes from either reliving the past or fretting about possible futures. (If you *must* worry about tomorrow, then at least give worrying your full attention, and get it out of your system!)

When we live in the moment, putting our heart and soul into whatever we are doing – drinking tea, smelling a rose, listening to music, making love, meditating, washing the dishes – we begin to realise our true potential. Heaven is here and now, in the ordinary magic of this moment.

Although every experience is unique, how often do we deny this? How often do we think 'This is just another cup of tea, like thousands I've drunk before' or 'just another evening at home' or 'just another day at work'? At weekend workshops, I often ask people to complete a task overnight, which we discuss on the following day. Invariably, someone will say, 'I knew what would happen when I did this' or 'I've done this sort of exercise before, so I didn't bother.' It is always sad to hear such comments. We might as well say that we've seen a sunset before, so why bother looking at any more? Or that we meditated once five years ago, so why do it again? There is incredible richness in each and every experience – if we allow ourselves to be fully awake, fully present. As Dan Millman[3] puts it, there are no ordinary moments.

In the film *Thelma and Louise*, two women take a short break from their run-of-the-mill lives. Thelma is a bored and unhappy housewife; Louise works as a waitress. In a drunken encounter outside a bar, Thelma is threatened with rape – and Louise takes out her gun, and shoots the aggressor. Suddenly, the women are wanted for murder. They are on the run. Driving towards the Mexican border, forced to live by their wits, and to abandon their former lives, they begin to come fully alive, and to discover their hidden strengths and potential. 'Are you awake?' asks Thelma, as they speed across the desert at dawn. 'I feel awake. I don't ever remember feeling this awake . . . Everything looks different.'

'Waking up' is such a precious gift that we can be terrified of losing it. Sylvia had a spiritual awakening at the age of thirty, after developing a potentially fatal blood disease. Together, we explored why she had become ill, and how she might recover her health. On an inner journey, Sylvia met a black hooded figure who told her that if she became well, she might 'fall asleep' again – and that it was not worth the risk. Sadly for those left behind, she died a year later.

LIVING IN THE MOMENT

As you sit, right now, become aware of your surroundings. Even if the room is familiar, look around as if you had never seen it before. Enjoy the different colours and designs, the textures

and surfaces, the patterns and shapes. Really
look. Can you feel the magic of this moment?
What can you sense right now? Perhaps the
weight of your body against the chair, the
sensation of your clothes against your skin, the
cool smoothness of the book jacket against your
fingers? Can you feel the magic? What can you
hear right now? A clock ticking, birds singing,
traffic passing by? Can you feel the magic? What
are you feeling right now? What can you smell?
What can you taste? Look at your shoe, or sock,
or bare foot – can you feel the magic? Can you
feel the magic of simply being alive in this
moment – living in the midst of this three-
dimensional theatre that we call planet Earth?

How often are you as fully 'awake' as this?
How often do you feel the magic of each
moment?

THIS IS IT!

A common way of 'waking up' to the ordinary miracles is to face crisis or tragedy. Bereavement, loss and
serious illness can all come as helpful reminders that
life does not go on forever, that we must cherish each
moment. Hilary, a thirty-nine-year-old secretary,
discovered a year ago that she had breast cancer.
Since then, she says, she no longer frets over finding
dirty socks on the bathroom floor, or missing a
favourite TV show. What matters most is spending
'quality time' with her family and friends, walking
down to the river, tending the garden. Simple things.

'Life has become much simpler, but somehow it's in sharp focus. The days used to blur into one another – but now, every day is precious and unique. Having faced the possibility that I would never see a daffodil again, I burst into tears of joy and gratitude when they came into bloom a few weeks ago – and I touched their petals with such tenderness. I'm not sure I had ever really *seen* a daffodil before.'

Shamans have long spoken of death as the wise advisor. Facing our own mortality, or that of others, can force us to reassess our priorities, and remember that life is not a dress rehearsal. This is it! There is not an endless supply of 'tomorrows' and 'next years'. If we miss an opportunity, we might never have the chance again.

A friend of mine, Sam, had been planning to spend a weekend with his parents. They had always longed to travel, and Sam intended to surprise them with air tickets. He decided to postpone his trip at the last minute, because of pressure at work – and arranged a later date. A few days later, Sam received a phone call at work. His father had died from a heart attack. Suddenly work didn't seem so important, and Sam took a week's leave to support his mother and arrange the funeral.

A similar lesson can come in much gentler forms. At the age of nineteen, I visited Pisa while touring Europe. Since I was on a tight budget, I decided not to pay the small entrance fee to climb the famous Leaning Tower. 'I'll return to Italy another year,' I told myself. Shortly after that, the Tower was pronounced unsafe and closed to the public – so I probably missed my one and only chance. It was a simple lesson, but I have never forgotten it.

FACING YOUR DEATH

1. How do you *expect* to die? How old do you expect to be? Who do you expect to be with you? Are these expectations based upon your family history, health statistics or some other source? Write down this 'programmed death', and flush it down the toilet as a symbol of releasing it.

2. Now, how would you *choose* to die? How old will you be? Who will be with you? Looking back on your life, what will you be able to say with satisfaction? What will you have learnt? What qualities will you have developed? How will you wish to be remembered? Imagine your death scene as vividly as you can, in order to programme it as a probable future. Would you like to be buried or cremated? What instructions will you leave for your funeral? If you could write your own epitaph, what would you like it to be?

3. How do you feel about considering your own death? Do you feel sad, scared, excited, numb? Do you want to avoid this exercise? Are you aware that your time here is limited, that every day is precious? What is really important in your life? Do you live as if every second counts?

THE SPIRIT OF EVERYDAY LIFE

One of the challenges of modern life is 'staying awake' while faced with all the busy-ness of everyday routines. It's all too easy for our spiritual awareness to become relegated to Sunday mornings, or the occasional workshop, or daily meditation, or times of crisis, instead of being integral to every moment of our lives.

The more often we remind ourselves of Spirit, the easier it is to 'stay awake' all day, every day. Everyone needs to find their own ways of doing this, until staying awake becomes an unshakable habit, our natural way of being-in-the-world.

For example, you might keep asking yourself, 'What am I experiencing?' or 'Am I awake?' or 'What is the opportunity here?' or 'Where is the love in this moment?' Or you might briefly 'go within' several times an hour – whether you are in a business meeting, on a train, or in a crowded street – reminding yourself that you are a spark of God/dess, that all guidance comes from within, or that all happiness and joy lies within. Or use affirmations, 'bubbles of light' and other techniques. Or simply take a long, slow, deep breath.

If you have children in the home – or even if you only have an inner Child – it can be fun to adopt the Findhorn method of painting 'Love', 'Joy', 'Delight' and other soul qualities on mugs, giving names to your rooms, sticking little angels on the windows, and so on.

Another possibility is to connect with Spirit through everyday tasks. For example:

- Having a bath or shower can become an opportunity to 'cleanse' yourself of the past, or of certain negative beliefs, or to 'wash away' fears and doubts, or simply to release the day. ('As the water falls down upon me, let it wash away any fears and doubts in the day that lies ahead. Let its energy fill me with trust and confidence.')

- Washing dishes can be a wonderful opportunity to really look at the crockery you use every day, or to notice the miracle of water and soap bubbles; or to remember that washing up is an act of love for those who ate this meal – whether it is just you, family or friends. (Nothing is ever 'just a chore.')

- Every mealtime is an opportunity to remember that the Earth has given this gift of food, so that we can live upon her. Give thanks in whatever way feels right – and savour every mouthful. You could also light a candle for a soul quality, or for a global issue.

- Whenever you walk upstairs, you might affirm that you are reaching for a higher perspective on your life, that you are becoming your Higher Self. (Feel the shift in your energy.)

- Going downstairs, you can affirm that you will always honour your Basic Self – your emotions and bodily needs – or that you will keep your feet on the ground.

- Walking through doorways, imagine that you are passing through a fine wire-mesh screen, which will 'sieve out' your fear, or doubt, or self-pity, or resentment, or a past relationship, or whatever you wish. (You might find it best to allow every doorway to represent the same gremlin – perhaps for a week or two – until you feel ready to move on. Or you can choose a particular door at home or work to carry your 'screen'.)

- When shopping, you might give thanks for 'convenience shopping', which means that we need not spend our days gathering and preparing food, but have time for more varied and creative pursuits.

Tap into inner guidance over which foods to buy, trusting your gut response to each item you pick up. You might spend time standing in queues using affirmations; or looking for 'mirrors' in the people around you; or sending love and light to anyone who looks sad, grumpy or harried. It can also be fun to ask your inner guidance which queue will move most quickly!

- Whenever you glance in a mirror, it is a good opportunity to use an affirmation, such as 'I love you', 'You're a beautiful person', 'Today, I am open to miracles', or 'I am fully alive in each moment.'

- Whenever you go for a walk – even if you're just stepping into your car! – be aware that you are treading on the face of Mother Earth. You might give thanks for the beauty of the trees or sky or buildings, for the air that we breathe, for all that the Earth freely gives us.

While strolling in a forest one day, Spirit gave me the following chant, to be recited (silently or out loud) while walking. It is a 'call-and-reply' chant: each line is guidance from our Higher Self, followed by our own confirming response. I often chant it for a few minutes in time with my footsteps, dwelling on the meaning of each line, and find it a powerful way of staying centred in Spirit:

Walk in beauty – I walk in beauty.
Walk in joy – I walk in joy.
Walk in truth – I walk in truth.
Walk in love – I walk in love.
Walk in the remembering – I walk in the remembering.

It is fun to create your own ways of bringing Spirit into everyday tasks, to discover what works for you. It's also crucial to build up a support system of like-minded friends, to avoid feeling isolated, crazy or simply smug! (If you cannot find any kindred spirits, perhaps you believe that the spiritual path is a lonely one, or need to cling to feeling different or 'special'?)

It is worth noticing any situation where you are easily thrown off-centre, where you tend to lose your higher awareness – perhaps when faced with your boss, or when your children refuse to go to bed, or when your mother pops in unexpectedly, or at meal-times, or when your neighbour starts playing the electric guitar. Know that you are creating this situation as your latest challenge! How can you 'stay awake' in *this* situation? How can you maintain your inner peace, or sense of humour, in *this* situation? How do you remember that we create our own reality, or that the Earth is just a giant theatre, in *this* situation?

THE IMPORTANCE OF BREATH

A time-honoured way of 'staying awake' is to become aware of our breath. Breath is the spirit of life, and whether we feel energised or exhausted, emotional or numb, often depends upon how we are breathing. If we are avoiding the present moment, or suppressing any emotions, our breath automatically becomes shallow – and our energy flow is thereby restricted. Shallow breathing can become a habit, with the result that we are always semi-conscious, always semi-alive. (After all, if we suppress our breath completely, we become *un*conscious.)

It is a good practice to check your breathing several times a day, take a few slow, deep breaths, and perhaps yawn and stretch – to reconnect with your body and 'wake up' to the present moment. Here are a few breathing techniques which might help:

1. A good 'cleansing breath' is to breathe in (through your nose) as if pulling air up through your feet into your body. Blow the air out through your mouth, imagining that you are releasing any fear or tension, or any energy that you do not want. Breathe slowly and calmly.

2. Or try circular breathing – breathing in and out, fully and deeply and continuously, without any pause between breaths. (This can cause a wide variety of physical and emotional responses; just notice and stay with whatever happens. Remember that you can stop whenever you wish.)

3. A breathing technique I learnt in Hawaii is known as piko-piko. It has five stages:

    (a) Breathe in focusing on the crown of your head, then out focusing on your navel.

    (b) Breathe in the stars above, then breathe out the earth below. (Do this in whatever way feels right to you.)

    (c) Breathe in through your shoulders, then out through your hips.

    (d) Breathe in the horizon, then out focusing on your navel.

    (e) Focus on your navel.

    (A brief version of piko-piko, also effective in making one feel centred and 'present', is to breathe while focusing on the crown and navel simultaneously.)

4.   A method taught by the old Hawaiian kahunas is to breathe deeply, and imagine that a fountain is rising up from your lungs, and overflowing through the top of your head. (I find this very energising yet calming.)

5.   A shamanic 'four-fold breath' is to extend your abdomen so that air is *drawn in* to a count of four, then hold for four, then gently pull in your abdomen so that the air is *pushed out* to a count of four, then hold for four. Repeat this cycle four times in all.

6.   A Tibetan technique is to breathe in through the nose for a slow count of 8, hold for a count of 32, then breathe out through the nose for a count of 16. Continue for several breaths, without pausing between breaths. (This one is quite challenging.)

7.   Another method I use is to breathe in, then breathe out to the sound of 'Om', three times over. This is said to harmonise our physical, emotional and mental bodies.

8.   Finally, an approach I learnt from Emmanuel is to imagine breathing in the future, with all that you want to become and create – and breathing out the past, with all your negative beliefs and limitations. (This is an excellent reminder that the time is always Now – that we are always at this meeting point between what we call 'past' and 'future'.)

THE TOOLS ARE NOT THE PATH

It is crucial to remember that the tools and techniques of any Path are not the Path itself. We must not confuse the finger pointing at the moon with the moon itself.

My friend Tanya once lodged with a woman who rose at five o'clock every morning to chant loudly for two hours (while Tanya was trying to sleep). The woman would then grouch over breakfast about Tanya wearing out 'her' crockery, and sitting in 'her' chairs, before donning the clothes and beads of her spiritual sect, and grumpily wafting off in a cloud of incense to a job she openly detested! The woman had mistaken 'the finger pointing' – the chanting, the clothes, the incense – for the 'moon' of spirituality.

Spirituality is not about possessing the 'right' books, tapes, oils, crystals and native artefacts. It is not about meditating for hours each day, or wafting around looking ethereal. It is not about practising sacred dances and chants, attending impressive ceremonies and rituals, poring over ancient texts and knowing all the latest buzz-words. All of this *can* be useful, interesting, healing, inspiring and heartwarming. It can help us feel connected. It *can* help us to stay awake. But it can also be a vehicle for the Ego, creating the mere illusion of change. ('Just look how spiritual I am!') The tools, the techniques, the scriptures, the paraphernalia – all are just fingers pointing at the moon.

I think we should be wary of trying to 'become' a native American, or Tibetan, or Shinto priest – or anyone other than who we are. It's all too easy to get carried away with the exoticism of crystals, smudge sticks, oriental incense, foreign jargon, power animals and hypnotic chants, and lose sight of the *point* of it all.

True spirituality is about love – love for self, love for others, love for the planet. It is feeling committed to *being here* on the planet. It is *living* our love, our wisdom, amidst the challenges of everyday life. It is listening to our inner guidance. It is seeing the ordinary miracles. It is living with awe, with wonder, with faith, with joy, with gratitude. It is seeing God/dess in the eyes of a newspaper-seller. It is seeing God/dess in a lace tablecloth. It is seeing God/dess in a spider's web. It is knowing that heaven is here and now.

FINDERS, SEEKERS

One of the paradoxes of the spiritual Path is that we can become preoccupied with getting 'there', instead of focusing on being 'here'. Zen Buddhism teaches us not to seek enlightenment since it is like chasing one's own shadow. The faster we run, the faster it recedes.

As I see it, there are two aspects of the spiritual Path: finding and seeking. The Seeker within us might be seen as the 'masculine' side of our spirituality – the active, doing, goal-oriented, achieving side, which might devour books by the dozen, attend lectures and workshops, and ponder over esoteric philosophy. It is more concerned with details than with the whole picture. The Seeker is ever-hungry – always hurrying to get 'there', always reaching for the future.

Then there is the 'feminine' side of our spirituality – the Finder within us. The Finder lives in a state of Grace, gently rocked in a warm cradle of love, unperturbed by the choppy waves of everyday life. It whispers that there is 'nothing to do, nowhere to go' – that all is well, that everything is perfect, that we are unconditionally loved. It knows that there is no need to struggle, no need to search, that freedom comes from knowing that we are already free. ('What is the method of liberation?' asked Tao-hsin. 'Who binds you?' replied his teacher. 'No one binds me,' said Tao-hsin. 'Why, then, should you seek liberation?'⁴) The Finder within holds our inner peace.

I believe that we have to integrate Finding and Seeking, being and becoming, feminine and masculine – that both are necessary on the spiritual Path. Neither approach is 'better than' the other. It is a question of what suits each individual at a given point in his or her journey. Each of us has to find our own balance – but if we walk too heavily on one foot, we might end up walking in circles.

Some years ago, I had a powerful dream on this theme. In the dream, I am a guest at a weekend gathering at a large country estate. From the lounge, I notice a delicate, pale-faced woman with silver hair through the windows, almost floating through the sunny, expansive gardens in an off-white voile dress – but just as I feel the impulse to follow her, another woman comes over to chat with me. She is very practical, business-like, extrovert, wears a smart yellow suit, and has golden hair like sun-ripened corn. (I am particularly struck by the colour of her hair.) While Golden Hair monopolises my attention, Silver Hair drifts ethereally across the lawn and out of sight. In the next scene, there has been a murder: Silver Hair is dead. In classic whodunnit style, detectives inform us that no one should leave the house. I notice Golden Hair slip out of the room, and suddenly know – with utter certainty – that she is the murderer. I wonder whether to tell the detectives, then abruptly wake up . . .

In exploring this dream, I realised with some

horror that Silver Hair represented my inner female, who was being 'murdered' by Golden Hair, my inner male. (Silver = moon = feminine. Gold = sun = masculine.) The imbalance between my masculine and feminine selves had been a recurring theme for many years, but this was an urgent message!

Looking at my lifestyle, I could see that I was leaving little space for the feminine. I was forever busy running workshops, giving or attending lectures, seeing clients, doing inner work, writing, reading, doing administration – and even when I took time out for personal travel, I would dash about from one workshop or power spot or sacred site to the next. I was often too 'busy' even to notice the weather outside, let alone to sit and watch the squirrels play. How could I help people to live in balance, to honour their wholeness, unless my own life was in balance?

My masculine side had always been well-developed. I had a good intellect, and was physically strong, practical and independent. As an adult, I was constantly seeking new challenges, and became restless after a year or two in any job or place. I regularly moved to new cities where I knew no one, almost always choosing to live alone – and I loved to travel the world alone. I read voraciously, and felt driven to do, to achieve, to be productive, to be busy. Having grown up in a society which valued the 'masculine' and denigrated the 'feminine', I had learnt my lesson well!

Like Sleeping Beauty, I often imagined that happiness and enlightenment lay in wait – in the next book, the next workshop, the next relationship, the next city. I felt I was pursuing my ideal self like a runaway train, but that once I caught up with her, I would be happy and content. I knew *in theory* that the challenge was to love myself as I was, but in practice, self-love always lay around the next corner. I never felt worthy, never felt that I was matching up to my own high expectations, never felt that I had done enough, achieved enough, given enough, to be loved. I had brief glimpses of the Finder within – peak experiences, moments of bliss, times when I reclaimed my wholeness – but they soon passed. I was always on the run, always chasing rainbows.

As I began to balance my 'feminine' and 'masculine' energies – by spending more time in nature, giving higher priority to relationships, reading poetry, going to art galleries, travelling more, relaxing more – something strange happened. I came to truly 'know' that, with all my faults and shortcomings, with all my messiness and contradictions, I was doing fine! More than that, that *everyone* was doing fine! (As I heard a priest comment on the radio, 'God doesn't make rubbish.') There is no deficiency for us to make up. There is no original sin. We have not disappointed God/dess or our Higher Self. We do not have to earn love. We do not have to deserve love. We do not have to be 'perfect'. We are loved for our uniqueness. *We are loved simply for being*.

It sounds obvious now, but it marked a profound change in my life. I began to 'wake up' to the ordinary miracles. Instead of living for tomorrow, I learnt to cherish today. The Finder within me was stirring from her slumbers. The Goddess was awakening . . .

Of course, for some people, it is the Seeker which needs to be awakened. The Finder is the mystic within – the part of us which knows that we are One, and merges with the infinite. Unless this is balanced by the energy of the Seeker, the result can be apathy, or little sense of personal identity – someone who seems to be 'barely there', and is unlikely to cope well with the practical demands and responsibilities of everyday life. Our challenge is not to merge with the infinite; our challenge – while we are still on the planet – is to live with 'a foot in both worlds'.

BECOMING A SEEKER-FINDER

Relax deeply, then imagine that you are in a beautiful forest. It is the magic hour between sunset and nightfall, and the trees are becoming silhouettes against the pink air of twilight. Hush – listen to the forest!

Now look for a winding path which leads deep into the heart of the forest – and follow the path until you come across a temple. Notice the shape, size and colour of your temple. What is it made of? Notice the door of your temple – and step inside. (Your Higher Self and/or your guide might join you, or you might be alone.)

Now mentally ask your Seeker to come to you – the driving force, the dynamic mover, the 'masculine' energy within you. Wait patiently, until you see or sense a presence approaching from your right side. The Seeker might appear as a male figure, or a golden light, or in some other form. Trust whatever image comes to you.

Thank your Seeker for coming, and ask how well you are expressing its energy in your life.

You might hear words, or see images, or be given a symbolic gift. Ask for guidance on what your Seeker would like you to do. (Bear in mind that your Seeker wishes to be in balance. If you are forever Seeking, and never Finding, your Seeker might be angry at bearing such a heavy load, and never being able to rest.) Listen carefully as your Seeker gives you a message.

Now ask your Finder to join you – your 'feminine' aspect – that part of you which holds your inner peace, which knows that there is no separation between you and God/dess. The Finder might appear as a female figure, or a diffuse white light, or in some other form – probably approaching from your left side. Greet your Finder, and ask how well you are expressing its energy in your life. What would your Finder advise you to do – or stop doing – in order to balance your energy?

Finally, ask your Seeker and Finder to become integrated, helping you to find the right balance *for you* – for now – between seeking and finding. Allow them to merge into your body, one at a time, feeling the shift in your energy. (What do you notice about the difference in their energies?)

Remind yourself of what you need to do, or stop doing, to balance yourself. Then gently bring yourself back into the room . . .

To create a heaven on Earth, I believe that we need to integrate the Finder and Seeker within. We need the synergy of our 'feminine' and 'masculine' energy. We need the inner peace, joy and receptivity of our Finder *and* the dynamic energy and action of our Seeker. We need to live with awareness, wonder and gratitude in each moment, enjoying each step of our journey – while *also* recognising that it *is* a journey, that change is the process of life, that we must actively reach for our Dreams.

It is often said that before awakening, one chops wood and carries water, and after awakening, one chops wood and carries water (albeit in a different state of awareness). But this is only half the story! This is the Finder's awakening – the ability to see the ordinary miracles, to live in the moment, while being aware of the greater Reality. It is a state of grace which is a necessary *prelude* to becoming a Seeker at a higher octave.

The Seeker is like a grain of sand in an oyster, creating a mild dissatisfaction with 'what is', and thereby creating a pearl. The Seeker is not content to be a passive recipient of 'what is'; it strives for 'what can be'. When Finder and Seeker unite, the result is a visionary who is dedicated to growth and change, personally and globally – while also living with joy, and surrendering to the Great Mystery.

As we transcend the duality of Seeking and Finding, as we wrestle with the paradox and shift beyond it, we take a quantum leap to a new level of consciousness: that of the practical visionary, the mapmaker, the Dream-weaver, the co-creator, the world server. The desires for individuality and Oneness are reconciled, as we move beyond growth through struggle, and towards growth through joy.

'Waking up' can and should change our lives. It should make a difference. As Helen Keller said, 'Life is either a daring adventure or it is nothing.' We are here to create our personal and global Dreams – and we inspire others by 'walking our talk'. If we overflow with joyful exuberance, create what we want with ease, love and respect others, serve the world in ways that delight us, and honour our wholeness, then we pave the way for others to do so. If *we* sing, dance and celebrate our lives, we empower *others* to be bold, to be daring, to listen to Spirit, to follow their hearts, to discover their own uniqueness. Our task is to be loving and joyful. Our task is to be mapmakers. Our task is to step into the magic.

10

Adventures in Consciousness

*You will awaken from the dream, either now or later.
Why not now?*

(Bartholomew[1])

It was a sad and disturbing phone call. I had only
met Matthew once, but I had warmed to him immediately – and now he was dead. As my friend
recounted details of the road accident, I thought of
Matthew's girlfriend, and how she must be feeling. I
wondered why he had chosen to die, and mentally
wished him well on his journey. As the conversation
went on, I slowly became aware of a presence in the
room. Then I 'saw' Matthew by the window. He
was smiling, and holding a huge white daisy. It was
such an unexpected and strong impression that I
mentioned it to my friend. Suddenly the image
changed – and Matthew was sitting on the floor,
playing happily with a small dog. It made no sense
to me, but perhaps it was a message for his girlfriend?

The next day, my friend phoned again. She had
spent the evening with Matthew's girlfriend, and the
opportunity had come up to ask – rather gingerly –
whether a huge daisy or a small dog had meant

anything to Matthew. Indeed they did. Large daisies were his favourite flowers, and he did have a little dog. The dog's name was Daisy.

I am certainly not a gifted psychic, yet I have had countless such experiences, and firmly believe that everyone is psychic. Our sixth sense is a natural ability. The trouble is, most of us don't trust our intuition. We get brief twinges in our stomach, or 'hear' a gentle voice, or catch a fleeting impression, and dismiss them as imagination or heartburn. There are only two differences between 'psychics' and the rest of us: first, psychics devote time to practising their skills; and second, they *trust* what they 'see' and 'hear' instead of dismissing it.

As we approach the New Age, our growth is accelerating rapidly. Our consciousness is expanding collectively, and we are moving beyond the five senses. We are becoming multi-sensory beings. There have always been individuals who can readily see or hear spirits, sense colours with their fingertips, see auras, heal by touch, communicate with nature spirits and so on. In the twenty-first century, such abilities – and many more besides – will be accepted as normal. We are stretching beyond the limitations of the intellect and our five 'ordinary' senses, and beginning to discover our true potential.

There are countless spiritual Paths, all with their own strengths and weaknesses, all leading up the same mountain. Yet however much we draw upon ancient and modern wisdom, our own Path will still be a unique journey of self-discovery – a rainbow blend of whatever works for us as individuals. What is more, as we move rapidly towards the New Age, we have to create *new* ways, *new* paths, *new* approaches. The old Paths can only take us so far. If we are to move beyond the past, to reach towards our personal and global Dreams, to stretch the boundaries of human consciousness, then we must – at some point – take a leap into the unknown.

In this chapter, I offer a final pot pourri of multi-sensory skills and abilities, and ways of shifting consciousness. It certainly isn't necessary to develop all of the skills in this book. Focus on whatever interests and excites you, or whatever you seem to have a natural ability for. The only risk is that some people cultivate psychic skills with the aim of feeling 'special', or one of the 'chosen ones'! A healthier attitude is that we're exploring our potential, having fun, and developing abilities which might help to create a better world.

It is time now for *everyone* to become a shaman, a metaphysician, a dream-weaver, a walker-between-worlds – each in our own unique way. A shaman is a mediator between different levels of consciousness, and different dimensions of reality. Stepping into the magic not only means *seeing* the world in a different way, but also developing specific *skills* – such as shapeshifting, time travel, soul-linking, attunement with nature, manifesting, clairvoyance and sensing energy – all with the aim of *empowering* and/or *healing* oneself and others; all with the aim of creating a heaven on earth.

Life is an adventure in consciousness – and as Seth[2] said, consciousness is far more mobile than we think! Consciousness is not confined to the physical body. Although our consciousness might be *focused* in our human form, all consciousness is interconnected. There is no real separation between you and me, or you and a tree or rock, or between you and a 'dead' relative, or between 'you' today and a future 'you' in 2011 or a past 'you' in the twelfth century. Our separateness is an illusion.

The trick lies in allowing our consciousness to be mobile, while also hanging on to our sense of personal identity. In other words, to be an effective shaman, we must have a foot in *both* worlds. One foot is firmly planted in the physical world, while the other steps beyond space-time, beyond separateness, into the greater reality of Oneness.

EXTENDING OUR SENSES

Becoming multi-sensory starts by expanding our ordinary five senses – becoming more aware, more sensitive, to what we see, hear, touch, taste and smell. As we sharpen our ordinary senses, we expand our awareness and it becomes easier to sense the 'extra-ordinary'.

Why not put down this book for a few minutes and become aware of this room? Have you really *seen* everything in this room? Have you noticed the different textures, colours, shades and variations of light? What sounds can you hear? What can you smell? Touch a few objects, feeling the varied sensations on your fingertips.

Now stretch yourself a little further. Focus on the space *in between* objects, de-focusing your eyes. What do you see, sense or experience? Now notice how it *feels* in this room. How would you describe the energy or its impact upon you? Walk into another room, and notice any shift in energy.

Practise sensing energy *wherever* you are. What is the 'atmosphere' of this café, or train, or office, or house, or church, or supermarket – or in this particular *corner* of the café? How would you describe the energy of that person sitting opposite? Or the energy between that couple? Or the energy of that tree, or waterfall, or crystal? Notice *how* you sense energy. Are you hands or fingertips particularly sensitive to energy? Do you feel it in your solar plexus? Do you translate energy into images, or words, or sensations, or just 'knowing'?

SENSING AURAS

The aura – the energy field which surrounds and interpenetrates the physical body – has seven different layers (and more beyond that), corresponding to the seven chakras, with each layer interpenetrating the 'lower' layers. If we are able to see or sense auras, we can (with practice) assess the physical, emotional and mental state of a person, and where there are blockages which need to be cleared.

Sensing auras also allows us to observe the energy which passes *between* people. Several clients have assured me that they 'knew' their partner was having an affair as soon as they saw him in the same room as his lover. It wasn't his body language, nor noticing them make eye contact, it was just 'something about them' – the energy that invisibly passed across the room between them. Others have confessed to a fear that their partner might 'know' that they had slept with someone else. This isn't guilt masquerading as fear: a sensitive partner *will* know, by the change in the other's energy field, even if he or she doubts that intuitive knowledge.

The aura *creates* the physical body – rather than vice versa – and without it we cannot survive in physical reality. When the British comedian Tommy Cooper died of a heart attack on live television, many psychics had noticed his aura disappear, and knew that he was about to die. I remember Lazaris joking that if you're about to board a plane and none of your fellow passengers has an aura, switch to another flight!

It is easiest to sense the first three layers of the aura, since their energy is denser than the higher layers. The first layer of the aura – known as the etheric body – extends half to two inches beyond the skin. The second layer, the emotional body, is one to three inches wider than the physical body. The third layer, the mental body, is three to eight inches beyond the skin. The fourth layer extends six to twelve inches – and so on.[3]

SENSING AURAS

1. Put your hands up in front of you, with your palms facing each other, about 9 ins apart. *Slowly* draw your palms together until you sense a slight resistance. Move you hands back and forth slowly to check out this layer of your aura. (It might help to keep your eyes closed.) Now move your hands closer together, until they are almost touching – 2 ins apart at most. Sense the first layer of your aura here. (If you keep your eyes, closed it feels rather like hairs gently brushing against your hands, as the innermost energy fields come into contact.) Bring your hands even closer together without touching, and feel the *backs* of your hands bristling now, as the energy fields pass through your hands.

Now point an index finger at the palm of your other hand. Bring the finger closer until – without physically touching – you can 'feel' the finger on your palm. (Your finger should be about an inch from your palm.) Rotate your finger, and feel the slight tickle as a circle is inscribed on your palm.

2. In dim light, hold your hands up against a pale background. Gaze 'through' rather than at your hands, de-focusing a little, and you should see a haze around the edge of your hand and fingers.

3. I first learnt to see auras while attending dull lectures at college! Even when a lecture is interesting, it can be an excellent opportunity to observe the speaker's aura, particularly if they are standing against a light, plain background. Look 'through' rather than at the speaker, de-focusing your eyes, until you see the faint glow of the aura around their head. If you look directly at the aura, it will tend to vanish. Can you observe the size and shape of the aura? What is the predominant colour? Can you observe changes in the size, shape and colour(s) when the speaker becomes excited, or defensive, or intellectual, or heart-centred?

SHAPESHIFTING

Shapeshifting means taking on the characteristics or energy pattern of something else – whether a leopard, oak tree, waterfall, fire, rock, dolphin, spider or another person.

In its highest form, shapeshifting means literally *becoming* (say) a leopard or oak tree – that is, consciously shifting one's energy pattern until it becomes that of a leopard or oak tree. Myths and legends across the world are full of such tales of metamorphosis – such as the Greek god Zeus changing into a swan or a bull, the Hawaiian legend of the Menehune people turning into rocks, or the haunting Lakota legend of White Buffalo Woman – and it is said that some master shamans are capable of such a feat.

At a less advanced level, shapeshifting is a natural ability which we can all develop and use. I see it as an extended form of 'empathy' – in other words, the ability to put oneself into another's shoes, while also keeping an awareness of who one is. (The profession of acting evolved from shamanism.) We can shapeshift to gather information or a new perspective, or to heal and transform.

For example, two years ago my car failed to start one day. It had been 'coughing' occasionally for some weeks, but on this occasion, it simply wouldn't start. I eventually gave up, walked to my appointment, and some hours later tried to start the car again. No luck. So I went indoors, and shapeshifted. I entered a 'spirit body', and floated out to my car. As I mentally entered the car, and settled into the engine, I became aware of a pipe which appeared to be blocked by something thick and black. I imagined pelting the blackness with energy, and it began to disperse, breaking into tiny pieces. When the energy felt clear again, I moved out of the car, and re-entered my physical body. I walked straight out to the car – and as soon as I turned the ignition, the engine roared into life!

Everything is energy, and all energy is inter-connected, so we *can* have an impact upon anyone and anything, by shifting our consciousness. Of course, some energy patterns are more malleable than others – water is more malleable than a stone, for instance – so I assume that it's easier to clear an engine blockage, say, than it would be to repair a puncture. Theoreti-cally, it's *possible* to mend a puncture by shapeshifting but it's probably more sensible to take the tyre to a garage! (I remember an Aborigine medicine woman saying that modern Aborigines use telepathy only when they cannot use a telephone. Shamanism has always been an eminently practical approach to life!)

Shapeshifting can be used for many different purposes: to locate a lost person or animal, to 'tune in to' someone who needs healing, to repair a machine, to affect the weather, to change one's mood or energy, to receive guidance . . . Its uses are only limited by our imagination.

SHAPESHIFTING

1. Choose one or more of the four elements – Fire (for passion, vitality), Water (for emotionality, going with the flow), Air (for ideas, flexibility, clarity of thought), or Earth (for grounding, stability).

Relax, attune to Spirit – then imagine you are in a natural landscape. Use all your senses to find yourself there. Now search for your element – perhaps a bonfire, or a forest stream, or a gentle breeze, or a mountain. Imagine your body is becoming lighter and lighter, until it is barely there – you are almost pure energy, pure consciousness – then step inside the Fire, Water, Air or Earth. *Become* that element – perhaps changing from a breeze to a gale to a tornado and back again, or following the stream to the river to the ocean to evaporated moisture to raindrops and back down to the stream. Absorb the energy of that element – then step back into your spirit body, and allow yourself to become denser again. Then gently come back to the room.

2. Choose an issue or decision over which you would like guidance. Now choose someone – living or dead, real or fictional – whom you wish to consult. Relax deeply and imagine that you are in a place which seems appropriate to that person. (For example, beside a moonlit waterfall for the goddess Diana, or in the White House for Abraham Lincoln.) Or just choose a natural landscape. Mentally ask that person to join you, thank them for coming and ask permission to enter their energy pattern. Now step inside that person's body – and *as that person*, consider the issue or decision. Notice how your perspective has changed, and allow yourself to come up with unexpected insights or advice. Then step out again – and gently come back to the room.

3. Choose a close friend or loved one who would not object to being 'spied upon'. At a time when you do not know where that person is, or what they are doing, relax deeply and attune to Spirit. Now imagine that you are stepping out of your body and searching for the 'energy pattern' of your friend or loved one, rather like a homing pigeon. Trust that you know how to 'track consciousness' in this way. When you seem to have found and 'settled into' the other person's body, begin to open your inner senses. Where are you? What are you doing? What can you see, hear, smell, touch, taste? How do you feel? Gather as much information as you can – then return to your own body, and gently come back to the room.

Make notes on your findings, and later check out how accurate you were, telling your friend what time you 'dropped in'. (Before using this exercise, I suggest that you *either* arrange a time with your friend first *or* mentally ask permission, and state that your friend can protect their privacy if necessary.) Keep practising until your accuracy increases.

TIME TRAVEL

When I was five years old, I had a frightening vision. While standing in the bathroom of our family bungalow, I 'saw' soldiers in drab brown uniforms marching into a village, and 'heard' the rhythmic tramping of their heavy boots. Around me, there were huts built of dried mud and stones with thatched roofs. Dark-skinned people were screaming and running in panic, and I knew that our village was doomed. As a small child, I was paralysed with terror. As the vision faded, I ran to my mother in the kitchen, clutched her knees and cried, 'The soldiers are coming! The soldiers are coming!' My mother comforted me – but it was many years before I realised that I had experienced a past-life flashback that day.

The Basic Self carries all of our memories from other lifetimes – and fragments of these memories can be triggered by people, places or events which echo down the ages, or simply by reaching the same age as when a past-life trauma occurred.

Since the Basic Self is our body-mind, past-life memories can often be accessed through physical impulses, fears and characteristics. For example, I grew up with a strong impulse to make the sign of the cross, and to prostrate myself at church altars – a throwback to being nuns and monks several times over! Similarly, my shins have always been inordinately sensitive – and I discovered that my shins had once been deliberately smashed to pieces as a 'punishment' for astral travel (journeying out of the body). Many people have birthmarks which indicate fatal wounds from another lifetime.

Although I remember thirty or so of my past lives, I do not advocate delving into the past simply for the sake of curiosity – partly because it can become a way of escaping from being *here*, in *this* lifetime. However, there are three good reasons for exploring past lives.

First, it can help us understand and resolve fears and blockages which do not 'make sense' in terms of our current lifetime (such as the common fear of developing psychic or healing powers). Second, it is a way of tapping into wisdom, skills and abilities gained in other lifetimes. (As a metaphysical teacher, I can draw upon my experience as shaman, yogi, oracle, witch, priest and seer in other lifetimes.) Third, an awareness of other lifetimes expands our sense of who we are – reminding us of the multidimensional nature of our oversoul, reminding us that this current lifetime is just one of many roles we have chosen to play.

Many people are drawn to visit places where they have lived 'before'. Even if we have no conscious memories, healing can take place as we reconnect with another fragment of our wholeness. When I first visited Iona, on the West coast of Scotland, I stepped off the ferry and was enveloped by a huge, soft voice which said 'Welcome back.' I immediately dissolved into tears, and although only vague memories came to me, I felt more 'whole' for having stayed there.

In Northern Thailand, similarly, I entered a Buddhist temple in Lamphun, and unexpectedly burst into tears. As I knelt in the deserted temple, 'memories' flooded back of being a young boy who was educated in this monastery. The boy dearly loved Lamphun and his family – but he was sent away (possibly to fight the Burmese) as a very young man. He had never returned, and I felt his deep longing and nostalgia. By following my strong urge to visit this remote temple, I felt that I had somehow 'completed a circle', returning in another body to the place 'I' had once loved.

Sometimes we repeat an experience from another

lifetime – perhaps in a milder form – in an effort to jog our memory. For example, Bartholomew[4] told me that I had drowned in the South Pacific in a past lifetime, after training in the Huna wisdom. I did not mention to Bartholomew that I had trained in shamanism in Hawaii in this lifetime – and similarly, had nearly drowned in the ocean (see Chapter 1).

Children often recall past lives spontaneously, unless their comments are ignored or ridiculed. A friend of mine was once asked by her eight-year-old son, 'Mummy, I haven't always had this body, have I?' And a client recalled that, as a small child, she refused to eat porridge on the grounds that she didn't like it. Her mother asked the familiar question, 'How do you know if you haven't tried it?' – to which the little girl replied, 'I ate it when I was a teenager!'

One risk with past-life recall is that we might use the past as an excuse. ('I'm scared of flying because I died as a bomber pilot, so now I only travel by road and sea.' 'I'm suffering now because I have karmic debts from Atlantis.' 'I'm cruel to my son because he murdered me in the American Civil War!') The past never *causes* what is happening now, or we would be victims. The present moment is always our point of power. The past has *impact* upon us, but *we* make the choices, here and now.

What is more, the past is not fixed – any more than the future is fixed. We have countless probable pasts and probable futures, all of which already exist – and which constantly shift and change, like a kaleidoscope, according to our beliefs and choices *right now*. We *can* and *do* heal the past, in this and other lifetimes, often without being aware of it. We can also drop any negative karma – by choosing to learn the lessons, by forgiving ourselves, or by changing our 'past' choices. Everything is flexible. Everything can be healed. Everything is open to change.

It is quite easy nowadays to access past life memories. It is often enough to ask, wait patiently, and trust the answer that comes – whether as vague impressions, images, words or just 'knowing'. My brother was once asked by a sceptical friend, 'OK, where have you and I known each other before then?' Without thinking, my brother found himself saying, 'We fought in the Battle of Culloden.' His friend was somewhat stunned. Unknown to my brother, he had been obsessed with the Battle of Culloden since childhood.

Of course, our rational mind tends to cast doubt upon intuitive knowledge; but unless we 'remember' being a famous historical figure (and even then, *someone* had to be Cleopatra!), the vast majority of our past life memories are authentic. (And even if we *did* 'make it up', *what* we chose to make up would be meaningful and interesting.) The shaman does not make arbitrary distinctions between what is real and what is unreal. Life is a dream. Everything is real, or everything is imaginary, depending upon how you see it!

EXPLORING PAST (OR FUTURE) LIVES

First choose a focus for your exploration – such as understanding a fear or blockage, or tapping into knowledge or skills gained in other lifetimes, or tracing the karmic history of a personal relationship, or remembering whether you have lived in a certain place or certain period of history.

Relax deeply, and imagine that you are breathing in white or golden light, slowly filling your whole body with light. Now imagine that you are at the bottom of a huge staircase, and walk up the staircase, step by step, until you reach the top. You find yourself surrounded by a fine silvery mist.

Now begin to descend again – going down into another body, in another time and place. When you reach the bottom of the staircase, the mist begins to clear and you look down at your feet. What are you wearing on your feet? Are you male or female? Young or old? Open your inner senses, allow the scene to unfold, mentally ask whatever questions you wish to ask – such as who or where you are – trusting the answers that come to you.

If appropriate, you might wish to absorb the energy of that past (or future) life. Mentally ask to absorb that other self's wisdom, skills or personal qualities into your mental then emotional energy-bodies, and finally into your physical body and DNA. Or you might wish to *change* an event from that lifetime – in other words, shift into another probable past or future – by vividly imagining a different decision or outcome, in as much *detail* and with as much *emotion* as possible. Or you might wish to send love or healing to this past (or future) self, or ask your guide to help release you from the impact of this other lifetime.

When you are ready, affirm that you are now

returning to this lifetime – or climb up and down the staircase again – then slowly and gently return to the room.

(This journey is available on my *Exploring Past Lives* tape.)

SENDING LIGHT TO YOUR PAST (OR FUTURE) SELF

1. Think of one or more times in the past when you were in pain or confusion, or facing uncertainty and indecision. (If there are any episodes which still come to mind occasionally, you are still leaking energy to those past selves, and need to send healing light.)

Attune with Spirit, then imagine your past self. See or sense yourself as you were, and surround that past self with a circle of healing light. You might see the circle of light, or just sense or imagine it. It might be white, blue, pink, gold, violet or green light – whatever colour feels right. Send love into the circle of light, sending love to that past self, and give any message of hope, reassurance or inspiration which feels appropriate. Continue until you sense that your past self has received the healing, and is feeling more positive.

2. If you are having a difficult time now, put a note in your diary for later this year – perhaps six months from now – to remember to send a circle of healing light to your 'past' self of today. And make sure you do so when the time comes around!

3. You can use the same technique to send light to your *future self. Think of a time in the week, month or year ahead when you are likely to need support, inspiration or love, and mentally surround that future self in a circle of light. Similarly, one can* receive help and guidance from a future self – for example, by tapping into probable futures in which you made two different decisions, to see which outcome you prefer; or by meeting your 'highest possible self', absorbing its high vibrational energy, and asking for guidance. (An inner journey to meet your Future Self is available on my *Listening to the Whispers* CD.)

TELEPATHY

Telepathy is universal. We are constantly sending and receiving messages to and from one another, whether or not we are consciously aware of it. (This is one reason why city life can be stressful; we are bombarded with so much information, and can feel overloaded without knowing why.) None of our thoughts and feelings is really hidden, however much we might try to disguise them.

Many cultures, past and present, have used telepathy in a routine way. Tahiti became well-known for its 'coconut radio', in which news was transmitted telepathically around the island. Whenever early visitors came upon a new village, they were always expected!

According to the Huna wisdom, everyone and everything is connected by 'aka threads' – invisible cords of energy, which are connected in the solar plexus area. Close friends have much stronger aka threads than strangers who have just exchanged glances, so telepathy is easier between friends and loved ones.

Since it is the Basic Self which sends and receives telepathic messages, the task of the Conscious Self is: first, to give clear, perhaps written directions ('I'd like Mary to contact me urgently', 'Send my love to Uncle Fred in hospital'); second, to empower the Basic Self (build up 'mana' or power), perhaps through breathing, relaxation or feeling love for the other person; and finally, to 'get out of the way' and trust the Basic Self to do its job. (Since aka threads transcend time and space, it makes no difference whether the other person is next door, or a thousand miles away.)

With practice, we can send and receive more complex messages – but begin by sending love, or asking someone to get in touch. (How often have you thought of someone, then the phone rings – and guess who it is!) Then move on to 'tuning in to' a loved one to see how he or she is, receiving the answer as words, images or sensory impressions.

As any therapist knows, another person can not only send thoughts, but can also 'dump' emotion – as when a client or friend walks out of the door (or puts down the phone) feeling wonderful, and one instantly feels as though kicked by a mule in the solar plexus! This is because 'unwanted' emotions have been transmitted along the aka threads.

An old shamanic remedy for this is to imagine a

cord of energy between you and the other person, joining your solar plexus to theirs, then to bring down your hand as if it were a knife cutting that cord. Do this with the firm *intention* of breaking any emotional leakage from the other person. (One can unobtrusively use this technique in business meetings and many other settings.) If emotion has been 'dumped' in a room, clapping your hands energetically is a simple but effective remedy.

SEALING YOUR AURA

(This is a useful technique for 'sealing out' negative energy from other people and places. As we become more sensitive to energy, it is common to feel disturbed by large crowds or tense atmospheres, and we need either to 'close down' our auric field, or learn to harmonise the energies by keeping our own vibrations high. Strictly speaking, sealing your aura is part of the 'warrior' tradition, but I still find it useful on occasions! Sometimes I just weave light around myself in a continuous swirling motion, which seems to be just as effective.)

Relax deeply, with your eyes closed. Now imagine a shaft of golden light entering the top of your head. As you breathe in, breathe in this golden light, right down to your heart and solar plexus. Breathe in to a count of 3, hold for 3, breathe out to a count of 4, and hold for 4. Sense the power building in your body as you breathe in for a few minutes.

Now imagine your aura, like an egg-shaped cocoon surrounding your body. As you breathe out, imagine that the energy ('mana') you have been building up begins to flow out into this cocoon, filling it with golden light. Breathe *in* the golden light from above, and breathe *out* into the cocoon, in the same rhythm as before. Picture the outer edge of the cocoon becoming like a thick shell of transparent plastic, which will allow only positive influences to pass through into the cocoon. When the process feels complete, mentally affirm that your aura is now sealed.

WE ARE NOT ALONE

Sometimes people are confused by the apparent paradox that we create our own reality, yet other people and places can disturb, heal or uplift us. This is such a crucial point to understand. We create *or allow* our reality. If creating our own reality meant that no one and nothing could have any impact upon us, or vice versa, then the world would be a very lonely place. When Spirit created the world, one of the rules was that the individual sparks of Light, the multitude of beings in the mineral, plant, animal, devic and human kingdoms, *could have impact* upon one another. We are all connected. We can and do have impact upon each other, and upon the planet (within our illusion of separateness).

This only serves to *increase* our responsibility. If we are ever deliberately hurtful, dishonest or manipulative, then – yes – the other person did at least *allow* us to behave in that way, but *we* made the choice. The responsibility is ours, and our actions have an impact. If we destroy the topsoil of our planet through intensive farming then – yes – the Earth has 'allowed' us to do so; but *we* made the choice. The responsibility is ours – and our collective actions will have consequences.

As modern physics has shown, there are no observers in the world, only participants. Everyone and everything has an impact – even the flap of a butterfly's wing! Our only choice is what *kind* of impact we wish to have.

The fact that we passively allow rather than actively create some aspects of our reality does not mean that we are ever 'victims'. There are still reasons why we allow any impact – and once we become *aware* that a person or place is having an impact upon us, it is an opportunity to learn and grow. The responseability is ours. Why are we allowing it? What are we going to *do* about it? What *action*, if any, do we need to take in response?

THE IMPACT OF THE EARTH

Although most people accept that we can communicate (in some way) with animals and perhaps even plants, many would draw the line at the mineral kingdom. Yet in recent years James Lovelock's Gaia Hypothesis[5] has popularised the ancient idea that the Earth herself is a conscious being. According to shamanic wisdom, *everything* is alive. Rocks and crystals are conscious beings – the 'stone people', as

native Americans call them – albeit with a consciousness very different from our own; and the mineral
kingdom can and does have impact upon us.

For example, how many people have experienced
crystals apparently 'asking' to be taken home? At
London's Mind-Body-Spirit Festival, I once crossed
the huge exhibition hall in order to escape from an
expensive celestite crystal which had 'chosen' me.
However, I could still 'hear' a tiny voice yelling 'Buy
me! Buy me!' – and eventually I gave in!

Just before I ran a weekend workshop in Cornwall,
I felt prompted to visit an isolated circle of standing
stones known as Boscawen-Un. I found myself circling
the central quartz pillar repeatedly, dozens of times,
in a semi-trance. I knew that I was 'building energy'
– but for what? Suddenly I stopped, and heard a
deep inner voice say 'Let them come'; then I knew that
I was meant to do ritual work here. The next day I
brought my workshop group to the stone circle, and
everyone completed a healing ritual. It was a magical
experience for us all – enhanced, without doubt, by
the powerful energy of the 'stone people'.

As we become more aware of the impact of
earth energies, more and more people are visiting
sacred sites and power spots such as Avebury and
Stonehenge, Mount Shasta in California, Sedona in
Arizona, Delphi in Greece, Machu Picchu in Peru,
the Great Pyramid at Cheops, and countless other
sites. Whether it is the 'earth energies' and/or the
collective consciousness of pilgrims down the ages,
such places can recharge our batteries, harmonise
our energy, heal and uplift us, or even trigger life-
changing psychic and spiritual experiences.

Impact is a two-way process. Just as we can have impact upon the world, people and places can have impact upon us. We give energy *to* and absorb energy *from* everything around us. Everything is interconnected. Everything is One. As Krishnamurti put it, 'I am the world.'

Where we choose to be – and *who* we choose to be with – does affect our consciousness. It is far easier to keep our vibrations high if we choose to spend time *with* people and *in* places with 'high' (loving, joyful, harmonious) vibrations. And as we raise our own vibrations – as we 'squiggle faster', as Denise Linn engagingly puts it – we not only change our own lives, but also have a positive impact upon everyone we meet, just by being around them.

RAISING YOUR VIBRATIONS

1. Remember that everything is our friend, and send love to *whatever* you experience. If you feel fear, doubt, negativity, resentment or self-pity, *send love* to those thoughts and feelings, rather than rejecting or battling with them. Melt the thoughts and feelings in a warm embrace. Whatever comes up, send it love.

2. Notice what makes you feel joyful, expanded, at peace, loving and loved. Perhaps immersing yourself in inspirational music, or walking in nature, or sketching, or sunbathing, or pottering in the garden, or practising yoga – and devote time regularly to these activities.

3. Imagine brilliant white light entering the top of your head, and moving down to your heart. Your heart begins to pulse with light, like a star – then radiates light throughout the cells of your body. Feel your body pulsating with love and light. Then the light begins to spill out beyond your skin, surrounding you in a bubble of brilliant white light.

4. Relax, attune to Spirit, then ask your Higher Self to help you resonate to the frequency of joy, or love, or humour, or courage, or gratitude, or trust, or bliss – or whatever you choose. Enjoy!

MAKING YOUR HOME RADIANT

(If we live in dark, cluttered rooms full of knick-knacks and memorabilia, or stacked high with unwanted books and files, or amidst an ever-growing pile of washing and dirty dishes, it is not easy to think clearly, or to feel light, free and joyful.)

How radiant is your home (or workplace)? How could you make it feel more light-filled, clear, harmonious, soothing or energising? What impact does colour have on your energy or mood? Does your colour scheme feel right? Perhaps you would prefer a yellow study, or a pale green living room? How can you add to the sense of light and space in your home? Do you need to clear out any clutter – to throw out or give away furniture or possessions which are unnecessary, or tie your energy to the past? Which objects (or colours) lift your energy, and which seem to absorb energy? Have you noticed how it affects your state of mind if the living room is in a mess, or the wastepaper baskets are overflowing? What changes do you need to make at home?

MAKING CHOICES

The more we learn to shift our consciousness and expand our awareness, the more aware we become that we always have a *choice* about what to experience. Fear is a choice. Love is a choice. Doubt is a choice. Trust is a choice. Suffering is a choice. Joy is a choice.

In any moment, we can choose how to think and feel. One cold wet day in January, as I stepped on to the escalator at Highgate tube station, jostled by the rush-hour crowds, I remember longing to be warm, dry and peaceful at home. Then I reminded myself that heaven was ever-present, *here and now*. My consciousness immediately expanded – and I rode up the escalator in a state of pure bliss!

Life is an adventure in consciousness – and it is up to us to choose what we wish to experience, to choose our own adventure. Again, it's important not to get carried away by the glitz or glamour of metaphysics and shamanism, and miss the *point* of it all. We might gaze at auras, shapeshift and talk to dandelions all day long – but if we have forgotten how to *love*, if we

have forgotten how to live with *joy* and *ease*, then we
have lost the heart of our path.

THROUGH THE GATEWAY

Relax deeply, and imagine that you are
breathing in white light, shifting into a higher
and higher state of consciousness. Eventually,
you notice that you are surrounded by a fine
silvery mist – and as the mist clears, you become
aware of being in a mystical place. You are
greeted by an ascended master such as Jesus,
Buddha, St Germain, Kwan Yin, Merlin or
Pallas Athena or by another high guide, angel
or archangel.

The master leads you to a sacred pool of deep
turquoise, edged by white marble – and as you
step into this pool, you release the past. As you
dip your head beneath the water, baptising
yourself in the sacred pool, your past drops
away. All that is real to you now is the future.
You emerge at the far side of the pool next to a
thousand-petalled lotus, which unfolds petal by
petal as you gaze into it.

The master or guide now joins you again –
and asks whether you are willing to awaken
your light body. If you agree, the master will
work with your energy, triggering a cellular
realignment to your light body. You notice that
your body is becoming less dense, almost
transparent.

The master now hands you the Chalice of
Awakening – a golden chalice, filled with a sweet

elixir. As you sip from this chalice, you will awaken more fully to your higher purpose, and remember more clearly who you really are.

Now the master asks whether you are willing to pass through the Gateway. Are you willing to be a mapmaker, a dreamweaver? Are you willing to grow through love, joy, courage, trust and vision? Are you willing to be a role model for a new way of being? Are you willing to commit yourself to your spiritual path above all else? If so, see the Gateway now – huge gates surrounded by a swirling mist, with an undiscovered country beyond. Stand on the threshold of this Gateway, and consider your decision. Stepping through will mean committing yourself to a rapid path of evolution.

If you are willing, step through the Gateway – and experience the pure joy and ecstasy of this high dimension. (When ready, come back slowly and gently to your physical body.)

LIVING IN THE FOURTH DIMENSION

This is a decade of transformation, a decade of awakening. Personally and globally, we live in times of chaos and uncertainty, of rapid change and instability. Many of our political and economic structures, our institutions, our national boundaries, our former roles and stereotypes, are collapsing. Our old forms, our old structures, our old approaches, our old ways-of-seeing the world are dying – and we have yet to witness the phoenix rising from the ashes. More than ever, we need to have faith and vision. More than ever, we need to be willing to let go of the past.

At a global level, our vibrational frequency is increasing: we are 'squiggling' faster and faster. We are moving from fear to love, from doubt to trust, from limitation to potential, from problems to opportunities, from competition to co-operation, from struggle to joy, from conflict and polarity to harmony and integration.

Metaphysically, the Earth is shifting into the fourth dimension. Anything which still carries the energy of the third dimension – the energy of fear, struggle, conflict or imbalance – is now being shaken loose and thrown up to the surface. Personally and globally, whatever belongs to the Old Age now has to be healed or released.

In the meantime, our task as Light-keepers is to plant seeds for the future. As we move towards the twenty-first century, the past is having less and less impact; the future is what really matters. Our visions, our hopes, our desires – as well as our fears – now have a much more immediate role in creating our reality. Our visions of the future *will create* that future. It is our responsibility to see beyond 'problems' to *solutions*, to hold a vision of a future in which our personal and global challenges have been resolved. We do not need to know *how*, but we *do* need to hold that vision of hope and faith. We need to live *right now* in the fourth dimension – beyond fear, beyond doubt.

Growth through joy might sound like an easy option, but the reality is that it requires us constantly to face new challenges, expand our awareness, embrace our wholeness, take responsibility for our lives, tap into inner guidance, make steady commitments and actively reach for our Dreams. It requires us to give up our addictions to fear, struggle and martyrhood. It requires us to 'walk our talk' – all day, every day. It is not a path for the faint-hearted! It is a path for lovers of life, lovers of people, lovers of our world. It is a path for those who are willing to walk into the Dreamtime, to pass through the Gateway, to step into the magic.

This is a planet of free will. Although we have a chosen destiny – individually and collectively – we can move towards that destiny by choosing the soft, grassy path which runs by the bubbling brook, dancing together and celebrating as we go, or we can choose the stony path through the dark mountains and along narrow, precipitous tracks, feeling burdened and alone. We can walk unerringly towards our goal, we can amble down blind alleys, or we can take the scenic route. Whatever our path, we *will* get there, sooner or later – but perhaps not in this lifetime. The choice is ours.

At any moment, each of us has a choice about where to place our consciousness. Like a radio, we can tune it into any station we choose. We can listen to the voice of fear or the voice of love. We can grow through struggle and trauma, or through love and joy. We can walk in the shadow of doubt and unworthiness, or we can choose faith and trust. We can choose mundaneness and mediocrity, or we can dance our Dreams awake.

What is your choice?

Footnotes

CHAPTER 1:
A FOOT IN BOTH WORLDS

1. Robert Boissiere, *Meditations With the Hopi* (Bear & Co, Santa Fe, NM, 1986) page 14.
2. See my earlier book, *Living Magically* (Piatkus, London, 1991) for further reading.
3. Bartholomew, *Reflections of an Elder Brother* (High Mesa Press, Taos, NM, 1989) page 26.
4. Lee, Pali Jae and Willis, Koko, *Tales from the Night Rainbow* (Night Rainbow Publishing, Honolulu, 1990) pages 60–61.

CHAPTER 3:
OUR THREE INNER SELVES

1. For further details about the inner Child (and Adolescent), see my book *Living Magically* (Piatkus, London, 1991).
2. H.C. Moolenburgh, *A Handbook of Angels* (C.W. Daniel, Saffron Walden, Essex, 1984), pages 66–67.
3. For further examples of ritual work, I recommend Brooke Medicine Eagle's book, *Buffalo Woman Comes Singing*. See selected reading.

CHAPTER 4:
DANCING YOUR DREAM AWAKE

1. Lewis Carroll, *Alice in Wonderland* (Penguin, London, 1962).
2. The Seth books were channelled by Jane Roberts. See selected reading.
3. See my earlier book *Living Magically* (Piatkus, London, 1991), page 91. The cone of power technique is available as an inner journey on my 'Evening Tape'.
4. Bartholomew, *Planetary Brother* (High Mesa Press, Taos, NM, 1991) page 63.
5. Lazaris, 'Creating a Brilliant Future' tape. (See page 221.)

CHAPTER 5:
EVERYTHING IS OUR FRIEND

1. Sanaya Roman, *Personal Power Through Awareness* (H.J. Kramer, Tiburon, CA, 1986), page 104.
2. Frank Lake, *Clinical Theology* (Darton, Longman and Todd, London, 1966).
3. DaBen is channelled by Duane Packer. (See page 221.)
4. *Emmanuel's Book* (Bantam, NY, 1987), page 80.
5. Celeste (my own guide), 'Discovering Your Life's Purpose' workshop in May 1991.
6. Bartholomew is channelled by Mary-Margaret Moore. See selected reading.
7. A chapter is devoted to 'Listening To The Whispers' in my earlier book, *Living Magically* (Piatkus, London, 1991). There is also a self-help tape on this topic. (See page 221.)

CHAPTER 6:
BODY LANGUAGE

1. Deepak Chopra, *Quantum Healing* (Bantam, NY, 1989) chapter 2.
2. For example, see Lawrence Le Shan, *Holistic Health* (Turn-stone, Wellingborough, Northants, 1984). Originally published as *The Mechanic and the Gardener*.
3. Lazaris, 'Living Magically, Every Day' tape. (See page 221.)

CHAPTER 7: OUR UNSEEN FRIENDS

1. *Emmanuel's Book* (Bantam, NY, 1987) page 76.
2. H.C. Moolenburgh, *A Handbook of Angels* (C.W. Daniel, Saffron Walden, Essex, 1984), pages 47–48.
3. Amber Wolfe, *In the Shadow of the Shaman* (Llewellyn, St Paul, Minnesota, 1990), pages 53–54.
4. Sanaya Roman, *Spiritual Growth: Being Your Higher Self* (H.J. Kramer, Tiburon, CA, 1989), page 87.

CHAPTER 8:
MANY HANDS, LIGHT WORK

1. Marianne Williamson, *A Return To Love* (Aquarian/ HarperCollins, London, 1992) pages 190–1.
2. Anita Roddick, *Body And Soul* (Ebury Press, London, 1992), page 21.
3. Brenda Ueland, *If You Want To Write* (Element, Shaftesbury, Dorset, 1991), page 32. First published in 1938.

4. For further details, contact Lumin Essence. (See page 221.)

CHAPTER 9: MAGIC MOMENTS

1. Quoted in Benjamin Hoff, *The Tao Of Pooh* (Methuen, London, 1984) page 113.
2. Lecture in the 'Alternatives' series at St James's Church, Piccadilly, London, September 1991.
3. Dan Millman, *No Ordinary Moments* (H.J. Kramer, Tiburon, CA, 1992).
4. Robert Powell, *Zen and Reality* (Penguin, London, 1977) page 23.

CHAPTER 10: ADVENTURES IN CONSCIOUSNESS

1. Bartholomew, *Reflections of an Elder Brother* (High Mesa Press, Taos, NM, 1989) page 8.
2. Seth was channelled by Jane Roberts. See selected reading.
3. For further details, see Barbara Brennan, Hands of Light (Bantam, NY, 1988).
4. Private consultation, 1992. This Bartholomew is channelled by Joy Ballas-Beeson, P.O. Box 9002 #375, Boulder, CO 80301, U.S.A.
5. James Lovelock, *Gaia* (Oxford University Press, 1979).

Selected Reading

NEW AGE/METAPHYSICS

Bach, R., *Jonathan Livingston Seagull* (Pan, London, 1973).

Bach, R., *One* (Pan, London, 1989).

Bartholomew, *I Come as a Brother* (High Mesa Press, Taos, NM, 1986).

Bartholomew, *From the Heart of a Gentle Brother* (High Mesa Press, Taos, NM, 1987).

Bartholomew, *Reflections of an Elder Brother* (High Mesa Press, Taos, NM, 1989).

Bartholomew, *Planetary Brother* (High Mesa Press, Taos, NM, 1991).

Brennan, B., *Hands of Light* (Bantam, NY, 1988).

Carey, K., *The Starseed Transmissions* (Uni*Sun, Kansas City, MO, 1982).

Carey, K., *Starseed, the Third Millenium* (HarperCollins, NY, 1991).

Carey, K., *Return of the Bird Tribes* (HarperCollins, NY, 1991).

Chopra, D., *Quantum Healing* (Bantam, NY, 1989).

Dossey, L., *Space, Time and Medicine* (Shambala, Boulder, CO, 1982).

Ferguson, M., *The Aquarian Conspiracy* (Paladin, NY, 1982).

Fickes, B., *Ascension: The Time Has Come* (Council of Light, Mount Shasta, CA, 1991).

Gawain, S., *Creative Visualisation* (Bantam, NY, 1982).

Gawain, S., *Return to the Garden* (New World, CA, 1989).

Griscom, C., *The Healing of Emotion* (Fireside, NY, 1988).

Griscom, C., *Time is An Illusion* (Bantam, NY, 1989).

Griscom, C., *Feminine Fusion* (Fireside, NY, 1991).

Hay, L. L., *You Can Heal Your Life* (Eden Grove, NY, 1988).

Hay, L. L., *The Power is Within* (Eden Grove, NY, 1991).

Huffines, L., *Bridge of Light* (Bantam, London, 1990).

Klimo, J., *Channelling* (Aquarian, Northants, 1988).

Laut, P., *Money is My Friend* (Ivy, NY, 1989).

Lazaris, *The Sacred Journey: You and Your Higher Self* (Concept: Synergy, Beverly Hills, CA, 1987).

Lazaris, *Lazaris Interviews Book I* (Concept: Synergy, Beverly Hills, CA, 1988a).

Lazaris, *Lazaris Interviews Book II* (Concept: Synergy, Beverly Hills, CA, 1988b).

Millman, D., *Way of the Peaceful Warrior* (H. J. Kramer, Tiburon, CA, 1984).

Millman, D., *Sacred Journey of the Peaceful Warrior* (H. J. Kramer, Tiburon, CA, 1991).

Roads, M., *Journey into Nature* (H. J. Kramer, Tiburon, CA, 1990).

Roberts, J., *Seth Speaks* (Bantam, NY, 1974).

Roberts, J., *Adventures in Consciousness* (Bantam, NY, 1979).

Roberts, J., *The Individual and the Nature of Mass Events* (Prentice Hall, NJ, 1982).

Roberts, J., *The 'Unknown' Reality, Vol. 1: A Seth Book* (1st edn, 1977; Prentice Hall, NJ, 1986a).

Roberts, J., *The 'Unknown' Reality, Vol. 1: A Seth Book* (1st edn, 1977; Prentice Hall, NY, 1986b).

Roberts, J., *The Seth Material* (1st edn, 1970; Prentice Hall, NY, 1987a).

Roberts, J., *The Nature of the Psyche: A Seth Book* (1st edn, 1979; Prentice Hall, NY, 1987b).

Rodegast, P., *Emmanuel's Book* (Bantam, NY, 1987).

Rodegast, P., *Emmanuel's Book II* (Bantam, NY, 1989).

Roman, S., *Living with Joy* (H. J. Kramer, Tiburon, CA, 1986).

Roman, S., *Personal Power through Awareness* (H. J. Kramer, Tiburon, CA, 1986).

Roman, S. and D. Packer, *Opening to Channel* (H. J. Kramer, Tiburon, CA, 1987).

Roman, S. and D. Packer, *Creating Money* (H. J. Kramer, Tiburon, CA, 1988).

Roman, S., *Spiritual Growth: Being Your Higher Self* (H. J. Kramer, Tiburon, CA, 1989).

Sky, M., *Dancing with the Fire* (Bear & Co, Sante Fe, NM, 1989).

Solara, *The Star Borne: A Remembrance for the Awakened Ones* (StarBorne, Charlottesville, VA, 1989).

Wilde, S., *Affirmations* (White Dove International, NM, 1987).

Williamson, M., *A Return To Love* (Aquarian/Harper-Collins, London, 1992).

Zukav, G., *The Seat of the Soul* (Fireside, NY, 1990).

SHAMANISM

Brown, D., *Bury My Heart at Wounded Knee* (Vintage, London, 1970).

Devereux, P., *Shamanism and the Mystery Lines* (Quantum/Foulsham, London, 1992).

Eagle, M. B., *Buffalo Woman Comes Singing* (Ballantine, NY, 1991).

Eliade, M., *Shamanism* (Arkana, London, 1988).

Halifax, J., *Shamanic Voices* (Arkana, NY, 1991).

Harner, M., *The Way of the Shaman* (Bantam, NY, 1982).

Jamal, M., *Shape Shifters* (Arkana, London, 1987).

Kalweit, H., *Dreamtime and Inner Space* (Shambhala, Boston, Mass., 1988).

Matthews, J., *The Celtic Shaman* (Element, Shaftesbury, Dorset, 1991).

Meadows, K., *The Medicine Way* (Element, Shaftesbury, Dorset, 1990).

Meadows, K., *Shamanic Experience* (Element, Shaftesbury, Dorset, 1991).

Roth, G., *Maps to Ecstasy* (Mandala/HarperCollins, London, 1990).

Sams, J. and D. Carson, *Medicine Cards* (Bear & Company, Sante Fe, NM, 1988).

Walsh, N. R., *The Spirit of Shamanism* (Tarcher, Los Angeles, CA, 1990).

Whitaker, C. K., *The Reluctant Shaman* (HarperCollins, NY, 1991).

Wolfe, A., *In the Shadow of the Shaman* (Llewellyn, St Paul, MN, 1988).

HUNA WISDOM

Hoffman, E., *Huna: A Beginner's Guide* (Whitford Press, West Chester, PA, 1976).

Lee, P. J. and K. Willis, *Tales from the Night Rainbow* (Night Rainbow Publishing, Honolulu, 1990).

Long, M. F., *The Secret Science at Work* (Devorss, Marina Del Rey, CA, 1953).

Long, M. F., *Growing into Light* (Devorss, Marina Del Rey, CA, 1955).

Long, M. F., *The Secret Science behind Miracles* (Devorss, Marina Del Rey, CA, 1976).

Long, M. F., *What Jesus Taught in Secret* (Devorss, Marina Del Rey, CA, 1983).

King, S. K., *Kahuna Healing* (Theosophical Publishing House, Wheaton, III., 1983).

King, S. K., *Urban Shaman* (Fireside, NY, 1990).

Yardley, L. K., *The Heart of Huna* (Advanced Neuro Dynamics, Honolulu, 1990).

THE GODDESS

Edwards McVickar, C., *The Storyteller's Goddess* (HarperCollins, NY, 1991).

Eisler, R., *The Chalice and the Blade* (Unwin Hyman, London, 1990).

Goodrich, L. N., *Priestesses* (HarperCollins, NY, 1989).

Stone, M., *When God Was a Woman* (Harvest/HBJ, NY, 1976).

ANGELS

Burnham, S., *A Book of Angels* (Ballantine, NY, 1990).

Moolenburgh, C. H., *A Handbook of Angels* (C. W. Daniel, Essex, 1984).

Moolenburgh, C. H., *Meetings with Angels* (C. W. Daniel, Essex, 1992).

Taylor, L. T., *Messengers of Light* (H. J. Kramer, Tiburon, CA, 1990).

NEW SCIENCE

Bentov, I., *Stalking the Wild Pendulum* (1st edn, 1977; Destiny, Rochester, Vermont, 1988).

Bohm, D., *Wholeness and the Implicate Order* (Routledge & Kegan Paul, London, 1980).

Briggs, J. P. and F. D. Peat, *Looking Glass Universe* (Fontana, London, 1985).

Capra, F., *The Tao of Physics* (Fontana, London, 1976).

Capra, F., *The Turning Point* (Fontana, London, 1983).

Dossey, L., *Space, Time and Medicine* (Shambhala, CO, 1982).

Jones, R., *Physics as Metaphor* (Abacus, London, 1983).

Kuhn, T. S., *The Structure of Scientific Revolutions* (University of Chicago, Ill, 1962).

Russell, P., *The Awakening Earth* (Arkana, London, 1988).

Sheldrake, R., *A New Science of Life* (Paladin, London, 1987).

Talbot, M., *Mysticism and the New Physics* (Bantam, NY, 1981).

Talbot, M., *Beyond the Quantum* (Bantam, NY, 1988).

Toben, B. and F. A. Wolf, *Space-Time and Beyond* (Bantam, NY, 1983).

Zukav, G., *The Dancing Wu Li Masters* (Fontana, London, 1980).

Useful Resources

GILL EDWARDS
For a current brochure/newsletter of *Living Magically* workshops, self-help CDs, affirmation cards, music for inner journeys etc, please contact:

Living Magically
Undermount
Rydal, Ambleside
Cumbria LA22 9LT
Tel: (015394) 31943
www.livingmagically.co.uk

Single CDs currently include: Overcoming Inner Blockages, Healing Your Inner Child, Changing Your Beliefs, Healing or Releasing A Relationship, Soul Retrieval, Inner Peace, The Morning CD, The 2012 CD, Your Future Self, Healing Dis-ease, Your Future Self, Journey Into Past Lives, Wish Upon A Star (for children). **Double CDs:** Attracting a Soulmate, The Magic of Health, Creating Prosperity.

ORIN AND DABEN

For details of books, CDs and courses by Orin and DaBen (channelled by Sanaya Roman and Duane Packer), contact:

www.luminessence.com

LAZARIS

For details of the Lazaris material and workshops:

www.lazaris.com

HUNA

For workshops, books, DVDs, home study courses etc., on Hawaiian shamanism with Serge Kahili King (and others), see:

www.huna.org

Index

Bold entries denote exercises

Also by Gill Edwards:

WILD LOVE
Discover the magical secrets of freedom,
joy and unconditional love

Gill Edwards

In *Wild Love* clinical psychologist and
metaphysical writer Gill Edwards reveals a
deeper and more magical reality where you can break free
from the 'ego prisons' of fear and
guilt and start to love yourself, other people
and life, unconditionally.

Gill explains that your ego can short-circuit your
energies and make you always look for approval, safety or
control in your relationships. She explains that when we
learn to enjoy unconditional *wild* love, we will set ourselves
free to follow our dreams.

This beautifully written and inspiring book will
teach you how to change your life from the inside out, and
discover your unique potential.

978-0-7499-4001-0

PURE BLISS

The Art of Living in Soft Time

Gill Edwards

Pure Bliss is an indispensable handbook for the 21st century. Written by leading spiritual writer and teacher Gill Edwards, *Pure Bliss* helps us to abandon the stress, busyness and limitations of our everyday lives and discover a more carefree, joyful and creative state of being and living. You will learn how to:

- Tap into your inner wisdom
- Be more creative and productive
- Fulfil your peak performance
- Enjoy the simple pleasures of life
- Achieve inner peace

'Seldom have I seen such glorious ideas expressed so clearly . . . Gill Edwards has a special gift, a unique treasure, to offer humanity, and my soul sings its thanks to her every time I read a page of her writing' Neale Donald Walsh

978-0-7499-4005-8